GRUMMAN

21

TBF / TBM

"AVENGER"

AERO SERIES   VOL 21

GRUMMAN

TBF/ TBM

"AVENGER"

by

B. R. JACKSON and T. E. DOLL

ART WORK by JAMES DIETZ

ISBN–0–8168–0580–6

Aero Publishers, Inc.

329 Aviation Road
Fallbrook, California 92028

Commander Harry H. Ferrier, USN.

Printed and Published in the United States of America by Aero Publishers, Inc.

FOREWORD

Commander Harry H. Ferrier USN
Heavy Attack Squadron 123
U. S. Naval Air Station
Whidbey Island, Washington

March 6, 1969

I was first introduced to the TBF-1 at the Grumman Aircraft Engineering Company plant at Bethpage, Long Island, N.Y. in March 1942. Having been flying in the TBD-1 Douglas Devastator, I was greatly impressed by the appearance and capability of this new airplane.

I belonged to a detachment of Torpedo Squadron Eight that had been left ashore at Norfolk, Virginia. Our job was to receive the first TBF-1's and prepare them for combat. As part of that job we were at the Grumman plant to learn as much as we could about the airplane. There weren't any formal schools then such as we have today to learn about the systems and operation of new aircraft.

I won't attempt here to mention the performance and vital statistics of the airplane, these are amply covered in this book. Suffice it to say we were all looking forward to flying this magnificent new torpedo bomber.

After a very short, intensive training period we were ready to join our parent squadron, VT-8, aboard the USS HORNET in the Pacific. We left San Diego in May 1942 with 21 airplanes. Arriving in Pearl Harbor in late May we were called upon to send six planes to Midway Island. HORNET had already left to join the other carriers grouping to intercept the Japanese fleet.

The baptism of fire for the TBF-1 occured a few days later during the Battle of Midway. Five of the six aircraft were shot down in the first few hours of the battle, a rather devastating beginning. However, our efforts were not in vain as the attacks by the torpedo planes had upset the enemy's plans. The dive bombers were thus able to destroy the Japanese carriers while they were rearming their aircraft.

The TBF-1 acquired its name of Avenger from this battle. It went on to achieve a proud combat record during the remainder of World War II. I have always been proud of the fact that I flew on the first combat mission of this rugged airplane.

HARRY FERRIER

DEDICATION

When an author, or authors, begin to gather material for a publication on any aircraft, their quest for knowledge and research data finds them in correspondence with various aircraft companies. This task is sometimes difficult as many of the companies have retired from aircraft production, or personnel now employed have little interest or knowledge of older aircraft previously built.

However, on many occasions there is someone who remembers or has taken the interest in keeping historical information on hand.

One such person was Mr. Grant Daly, whose help and ideas in the presentation of this book were greatly appreciated. For Mr. Daly, who passed away in September 1968, we respectfully dedicate this publication.

The Authors

ACKNOWLEDGEMENTS

It is with deep appreciation that we the authors, Mr. B. R. Jackson and Mr. T. E. Doll, take this opportunity to thank the many people who offered their assistance in the publication of this manuscript.

Bunny d' E. C. Darby, Auckland, New Zealand

A. W. Cairncross, Sidney, Australia, AAHS

Col. Caldwell, USMC Historical Branch

CDR. R. N. Dahlstrom USN (Ret)

R. P. Gill, USMC Historical Branch

Lloyd S. Jones, AAHS

Jerry Kishpaugh, AAHS

W. T. Larkins, AAHS

A. W. Lawrence, USN (Ret)

Kurt Miska, Grumman Aircraft Engineering Corp.

National Archives and Record Center

A. O. Van Wyen, Naval Historian (Ret.)

Hideki Yamauchi, Osaka, Japan

Also special thanks to Mr. Grant Daly, to whom the book is dedicated and Mr. Gordon Crane, our proofreader, both deceased before the manuscript was completed. And last but not least, to Jo and Roz, our wives, ever patient and understanding.

AUTHOR'S NOTE

Unless otherwise credited, all photos are official United States Navy or official United States Marine Corps photographs.

TABLE OF CONTENTS

TBF-1's from USS Santee ACV-29, October 1942.

Chapter 1

THE INCEPTION

Grumman XTBF-1 mockup at the factory in late 1941. Note absence of dorsal fin.

In 1939 the Navy Department invited all United States aircraft companies to submit proposals for a new torpedo bomber design to replace the aging Douglas TBD-1. The TBD had become operational in 1937 and the Navy felt that its' usefulness was short lived and would seek an aircraft with more speed and an extended combat radius.

The Navy Department supplied each of the interested aircraft companies with a list of specifications as to the type of aircraft desired. Although a large number of proposals were received by the Department, only two were accepted.

The Chance Vought Company and the Grumman Aircraft Engineering Corporation's designs were endorsed as the most promising, and contracts were issued to each for two experimental aircraft. Grumman's contract, dated 8 April 1940, called for two aircraft to be designated XTBF-1. Vought's contract, dated 23 April 1940, called for two aircraft to be designated XTBU-1. The similarity of the two designs, presented by two different companies, indicated that the Navy Department had been quite specific as to the type of aircraft it was seeking.

The Navy specifications called for a three man crew, the same as its predecessor, the TBD-1.

The crew consisted of pilot, torpedo officer or bombardier, and rear gunner/radio operator. The aircraft would have to be stressed for carrier operations and would also be readily adaptable to serve both as a scout plane and a horizontal bomber.

Grumman's model differed little from the final design which would later win fame in World War II. The XTBF-1's vertical stabilizer area was larger and did not have the dorsal fin. Vought's aircraft looked like a slender cousin to the XTBF-1 as it featured an elongated canopy with a rear turret similar to the Grumman type. Its vertical stabilizer was higher and rounded at the top, and the wings longer and more narrow than the XTBF's, were rounded at the tips.

The first prototype aircraft, BuNo. 2539, flew successfully on 7 August 1941 under the guidance of Bob Hall, Grumman's assistant Chief Engineer in charge of experimental work.

The months following saw the XTBF-1 undergoing a rigorous flight schedule designed to give the engineering department valuable information that would in turn be incorporated into the production models should the Navy accept Grumman's airplane.

Testing continued with BuNo. 2539 without

XTBF-1 taken 20 December 1941 at Grumman factory. Bureau Number 2540.

incident until 28 November 1941, when a fire broke out in the bomb bay during a routine flight. The crew had to abandon the airplane and it was totally destroyed in the ensuing crash. However, the second prototype airplane, BuNo. 2540 was nearly completed when this tragedy occured and would make its first test flight on 20 December 1941. XTBF-1, number two, was identical to the first airplane except that a dorsal fin had been added between the fuselage and vertical stabilizer for greater stability in flight.

Sunday, 7 December 1941, found the Grumman plant at rest. "Open House" was in full swing at Plant Two, and the public was getting a chance to see what an aircraft factory looked like on the inside. Buffet luncheon would be served at noon, and later in the day all eyes would be on the "new" airplane poised in the center of the assembly floor. It was, as yet, unnamed. However, the events of the day would give the airplane a name, for some 5,000 miles away the Japanese Naval Air Forces were attacking the United States Fleet at Pearl Harbor. It was decided that the airplane would be called the AVENGER, a name that would more than typify its role in the years to come.

The Japanese attack had an accelerating effect on the Navy's decision to choose a contractor to produce the model torpedo bomber. On 23 December 1941, Grumman received an order for 286 TBF-1 aircraft. The Navy had been impressed with the XTBF-1's performance during flight testing and evaluation. Production began im-

mediately and the initial airplane flew on 3 January 1942, and was delivered to the Navy testing facility at the Naval Air Station, Anacostia. Another star in the Navy-Grumman sky had taken its place.

The Vought design had also gained favor with the Navy but they were too occupied with the F4U fighter to start production on the TBU-1. On 6 September 1943, Consolidated Aircraft Corporation undertook the job to build 1100 of the TBU-1s; now designated TBY-2, "Sea Wolf".

The first Sea Wolf was delivered in November 1944, but due to production delays the contract was cancelled after only 180 were built. These aircraft saw duty only at training bases in the United States and were never used in combat operations.

Following the delivery of the first production TBF-1 to the Navy on 30 January 1942, things began to swing into full gear at the Grumman plant. Completed aircraft began to emerge from the assembly lines at a record pace and by the end of May, 85 Avengers had been delivered to the Navy.

The production aircraft was somewhat bulky in appearance. The TBF-1 was a fat and stubby airplane with a cantilevered mid-wing. The center section of the wings was a rectangular section, with an equally tapered folding outer section. The construction of the center section was all metal, with split trailing-edge flaps located between the ailerons and fuselage. The outer wings were operated by a hydraulic control system

Front view of XTBF-1.

¾ right front view of XTBF-1.

TBF-1 competitor in the air 1942. XTBU-1 never saw operational service.

within the cockpit and could be folded in a matter of seconds by the pilot. This was one of the outstanding features of the Avenger as it enabled the pilot to fold his wings while taxiing onboard a carrier. Many hours would be saved for the deck crews with this added feature, and landing operations could be speeded up.

The fuselage was a basic oval design with a circular cross section that tapered almost to a point. The fuselage was also of all metal construction.

The tail unit was a basic cantilevered type, all metal in structure, and located above the fuselage. The rudder and elevators were fabric covered with the trim tabs located in the control surfaces.

The main landing gear system was fully retractable as was the tail wheel and arrestor hook.

The power plant for the Avenger consisted of a Wright R-2600-B "Cyclone 14" engine. Its fourteen cylinder radial air cooled construction produced approximately 1700 horsepower at take-off. Performance rating called for a top speed of 271 mph at 12,000 feet, 269 mph with torpedo or bomb load and 251 mph at sea level. Cruising speed was 145 mph and the landing speed was 76 mph. Service ceiling was 22,400 feet with a rate of climb of 1,430 feet per minute. Combat radius was 1,125 miles with a bomb load and 1,450 miles for scouting missions. The engine was housed in a NACA (National Advisory Committee for Aeronautics) cowling and carried a Hamilton-Standard constant speed, full feathering propeller.

The basic dimensions of the Avenger were: wing span 54'2", fuselage length 40', height 16'5" and the total wing area was 490 square feet.

Armament consisted of one fixed .30-caliber machine gun in the upper portion of the cowling, firing through the propeller arc by means of a synchronation gear, one .50-caliber flexible machine gun mounted in the ball turret and an additional .30-caliber machine gun which could be aimed through a small portal in the window located in the tunnel, or bottom section of the fuselage. All of the TBF-1's and TBM-1's carried the same armament and in the later models of the Avenger, the .30-caliber machine gun in the cowling was eliminated in favor of two fixed, wing mounted .50-caliber machine guns. The ball turret was power operated and provided protection for the Avengers tail section. The torpedo officers position was directly behind the pilots compartment with an easy access to the undergun position if the need was to arise. Most TBF's were flown with this seat empty and the radioman spent all of his time in the "tunnel" position.

The cowling mounted .30-caliber machine gun carried 300 rounds of ammunition, while the .50-caliber machine gun in the ball turret carried a maximum of 400 rounds. The .30 caliber machine gun in the tunnel carried a maximum of 500 rounds. With the addition of the .50-caliber machine guns in the wings, the fire power and capacity was increased as these guns were able to carry a maximum of 600 rounds of ammunition.

The self-sealing fuel tanks were protected by armour plating and consisted of a center main in the fuselage with right and left internal wing tanks. Total capacity was 325 gallons. An additional fuel cell could be affixed in the bomb bay and carry an extra 212 gallons of fuel. An expendable fuel tank could also be carried in the bomb bay with a fuel capacity of 58 to 100 gal-

XTBF-1 with new marking adopted in January 1942, red and white horizontal tail stripes.

lons. The latter fuel system set ups were usually used for scouting missions when a longer combat radius was needed.

Bomb loads for the Avenger varied. It could carry either an MK13-1 or -2 torpedo, one 1600 pound bomb, one 1000 pound bomb, four 500 pound bombs, twelve 100 pound bombs, one 650 pound bomb or four 325 pound bombs. The number and assortment varied with the type of mission being flown and the target being sought. The Avenger, in addition to its varied bomb loads, was able to create a smoke screen with the adding of a special tank in the bomb bay and was operated either manually or electrically.

As the evidence of a possible war loomed over the country during the latter part of 1941, the United States Government ordered a curtailment of all automobile production. When war was officially declared on Japan by Congress on 8 December 1941, the General Motors Corporation virtually stopped production in all of its plants throughout the United States.

The work stoppage would leave thousands of people jobless and the plants and factories that used to turn out thousands of Cadillacs, Oldsmobiles, Pontiacs and Chevrolets would be left as a ghost town.

The management of General Motors felt that these plants, with their huge tool rooms and assembly lines, could be put to some use to aid the war effort.

The Navy Department was contacted by General Motors with the idea that some type of contract could be arranged. This drew a blank. General Motors then contacted several other aircraft companies as to the possibility of its making spare parts for existing airplanes. This also drew a blank. Most of the aircraft companies were already in production and were well established with sub-contractors.

Finally, one afternoon in Washington, D.C., the Navy Department arranged a meeting between the representatives of General Motors and Grumman Aircraft. The meeting was called in hope that some arrangement might be made to produce work for the idled General Motors plants. The General Motors people had entered the meeting with the thought that Grumman was interested in obtaining an additional sub-contractor to build spare parts for its existing aircraft. To the surprise of the General Motors representatives, Grumman was seeking additional space for the full scale production of entire aircraft.

A team of General Motors engineers made visits to the Grumman Aircraft plant in an effort to study the methods of aircraft production. In return, Grumman representatives visited the many different General Motors plants and began to assist in the enormous change over that was necessary. Redesigning the automobile plants would take an all out effort by everyone involved, for these plants would have to be completely revamped to undertake the massive wings and fuselages of airplanes. The change over seemed like an impossible task, but was soon completed and General Motors became the Eastern Aircraft Division; soon to become a giant in the aircraft industry.

Grumman supplied the knowledge in transforming the automobile assembly lines into aircraft assembly lines and rendered to Eastern the

In the air on 23 March 1942, first TBF-1 in landing configuration and de-icer boots on its leading edges.

required parts for the first ten bombers and fighters, now designated the TBM-1 and the FM-1.

Engineering and the assembly of the aircraft were the biggest problems that Eastern would encounter. Putting an airplane together was a far different task than that of assembling an automobile. To aid the engineering department at Eastern, in their quest for knowledge as to the assembly of aircraft, they created the idea of the "PK" ship.

The PK ships were put together at Grumman, inspected and passed by the Navy. However, these aircraft were fastened together with Parker-Kalon fasteners and could be disassembled or assembled with relative ease. The PK aircraft gave the Eastern Aircraft engineers and personnel, the information they needed for final aircraft assembly. In addition to the PK airplanes, the Navy also sent to the Eastern plants, two "dog ships"; one a bomber and the other a fighter. These two aircraft remained in a restricted area and were not to be worked on in any manner. Their purpose was purely for reference and observation and provided Easterns' employees and engineers with a picture of that which they were supposed to duplicate.

By the end of March, 1942, the Trenton plant and the Linden plant, Eastern components, had received their PK aircraft and parts. The engineering staff began to study the assembled aircraft and began to set up its assembly lines and tooling rooms.

Toward the end of the year the vast problems of assembly lines, tooling, production and engineering that had confronted the General Motors people had been solved and their factories began to deliver to the Navy the much needed airplane.

Many plants were involved in the Eastern complex — their breakdown is as follows:

At the Trenton-Ternstedt Division, New Jersey, the center of the fuselage assembly, including the canopy section, was manufactured. Assemblies from the plants at Tarrytown, Baltimore and Bloomfield were sent to Trenton for the final assembly of the completed aircraft. Once off the line these aircraft were sent to a nearby airfield where Trenton mechanics and test pilots put each plane through grueling tests before delivery to the Navy.

The Bloomfield, New Jersey plant produced the varied cables, wires, tubes, electrical and hydraulic assemblies for the Avenger and the Wildcat. In addition, they also produced such parts as the ammunition boxes for both aircraft as well as the huge star decals that graced the wings and fuselage.

The plant at Tarrytown, New York, produced the wings and cowling assemblies for the Avenger.

The plant at Baltimore, Maryland, produced the aft-section of the Avenger which included all the area from the center of the turret to the end of the airplane.

The plant at Linden, New Jersey, produced the

entire FM Wildcat except for a few parts that the Bloomfield plant manufactured.

Late in December 1943, the Trenton-Ternstedt plant delivered the 1,000th Avenger to the United States Navy. In addition to these they also delivered 180 Avengers to the United Kingdom.

The Avenger was a "good airplane" and there were few undesirable incidents in its early days to tell about.

The wheels failed to extend to a proper position for landing on one occasion and it had to be brought in on the belly, which was made easier by the grass runways of that time; the electrical turret produced some trouble, but this was to be expected with its highly-complicated mechanism, and was eventually corrected.

On a test flight from Trenton in November 1942, Eastern's Chief Test Pilot had an Avenger up for its first, but unofficial flight. Returning to the field, he had switched to his reserve tank. Nothing happened, no gas flow. He manipulated the switch, still no gas. He managed to return the Avenger to the field and landed without mishap. A check into the problem revealed that the fuel selector valve had been installed exactly 180 degrees improperly. When turned to the "on"

position, no gas would flow through the valve; turned to the "off" position, gas would have flowed.

This problem was soon resolved, but more would turn up. Commander Roy N. Dahlstrom, USN (Ret.), at the time a Navy-Factory representative, recalls.

"A little old lady at the Trenton factory was putting the decal that said "FLAPS" on the component that operated the landing gear and the decal that said "LANDING GEAR" on the component that operated the flaps. To show, at the time, how much faith the pilots put in decals, no serious problems arose; however, one squadron commander did ground his squadron on account of this and I had to make a trip to the NAS to straighten things out."

The little old lady was assigned to another position. However, she would return to haunt Dahlstrom.

"At a later date, again at the Trenton plant, we had one inspector (little old lady, previously mentioned) who had the job of inspecting the life rafts that were to go into the TBM. It was her job to see that they had all the proper gear that made up the kit. One day the line stopped and I

Checking out the first TBF-1 delivered to the Navy, March 1942.

TBF-1 on test flight over Long Island, 1942.

went to find out why. It seemed that the trouble was at the point where the life raft was being put into the airplane. I asked the inspector why she was holding up the line and her reply was, because the whistle that went into each raft could not be heard at a distance of 50 yards and the specs called for it to be audible at that distance. So she stopped the line because the whistle was not up to government specifications. Because the whistle was judged defective the whole life raft was rejected, and this caused the line to stop at that point. After determining the problem I wrote a deviation which in effect said; 'To hell with the whistle, get the line moving.' "

Several airframes were used for experimental engine testing; one had an R-2600-10 two stage engine installed and was designated XTBF-2; another had the updated R-2800-20 installed and became the XTBF-3 — it was the prototype for the Eastern model TBM-3.

Night fighter equipment including a radome on the right wing, was installed on one, and infrared lamps, purpose unknown, were installed on another.

The first COD (carrier-onboard-delivery) airplane was an Avenger, with the provision for personnel and cargo in the bomb bay. An Avenger

was also the first airplane to carry the ASW (anti-submarine warfare) radome.

In addition to the two original XTBF-1's, Grumman built 2,291 TBF-1's, the last being delivered in December 1943. Grumman then turned over to Eastern Aircraft the remaining production orders so they would be able to concentrate on the F6F Hellcat. Eastern built 2,882 TBM-1's (F designated Grumman, M designated General Motors), duplicates of the TBF-1 and 4,661 TBM-3's with an improved engine and special configurations. Eastern also built three XTBM-4's which incorporated a strengthened center section and a revised wing fold system.

In January 1946, eight models of the TBF and eighteen models of the TBM were in existence. The most important of these were the TBF-1 and the TBM-1, which were the original configuration; the TBF-1C and the TBM-1C equipped with two .50-caliber wing guns and the TBM-3 with its more powerful engine. Other configurations consisted of the -1CP and the -3P, special photographic reconnaissance versions equipped with a trimetrogen camera; the -1D and -1E, the -3C and the -3E special radar versions; the -1L and -3L with a searchlight mounted in the bomb bay; the -1J, -3J and the -3U utility versions; the -3N equipped for night operations; the -3Q equipped for radar countermeasures, and the -3W which was a special radar search version.

Late in 1946, under the code name of Cadillac I, the Navy began a series of tests to develop extended radar coverage for the U.S. Fleets. The TBM-3W was used with its huge belly radome that housed a large APS-20 radar scanner screen. With the addition of a radar picket plane circling over the Fleet there would be a vast amount of extended coverage. Also in 1946, the Navy was involved in research for better methods of anti-submarine warfare. The TBM-3E's designation was changed to TBM-3S and underwent extensive testing of various types of search and electronic gear. These two aircraft and the research developments that they helped to originate would later be incorporated into what is now known as the "hunter-killer" teams of the United States Naval Air Force.

In 1951 the Avenger began to fade from the limelight of the U.S. Navy. The once proud and famed aircraft was slowly being replaced by newer and more advanced airplanes of the day. A few remained in service as late as 1951; either as personnel transports or assigned to Reserve and training units. Several TBM-3's were still being used as mail carriers for the Fleet and Marine Headquarters Squadron. One had several TBM-3R's until the mid-fifties. The First Marine Air Wing, stationed in Korea operated approximately 20 TBM's -3E's and -3R's, but these were only a few of the many Avengers that had existed during the early and mid-1940's.

★ ★ ★ ★ ★ ★ ★ ★ ★

Chapter 2

THE PACIFIC

In March of 1942 a detachment of personnel from Torpedo Squadron 8, VT-8, was sent to the Grumman plant at Bethpage Long Island, to learn as much as possible about the TBF-1 from its engineers and designers. Meanwhile, the remainder of the squadron was enroute to the Pacific onboard the USS HORNET (CV-8).

At the end of the month, March 1942, the first of the new Grumman Avengers was delivered to VT-8 and a series of tests was started to train the remaining detachment. Mechanics, as well as pilots, began an indoctrination course that would enable them to relay valuable information to the remainder of the squadron when additional airplanes were delivered.

The detachment, based at Norfolk Naval Air Station, made high-speed torpedo runs at Quonset Point, Rhode Island, with a newly developed torpedo that could survive high speed drops at higher altitudes. This new torpedo was especially designed for use by torpedo bombers and could be dropped at a speed of 125 knots and between 125 to 150 feet. This new "fish" was a definite improvement over those being used with the TBD-1s.

After only a few days in which to familiarize themselves with their new aircraft, the detachment was recalled to Norfolk and ordered to fly the TBFs to San Diego. The other members of the detachment, less those transporting the aircraft to San Diego, would meet them on the West Coast, then proceed to the Pacific and rejoin the squadron onboard the HORNET.

From San Diego, the detachment was transported to Ford Island in the USS KITTY HAWK (AKV-1), a converted railroad car transport. The TBFs were unloaded and preparations were started to ready them for sea duty. Shortly after their arrival, a call went out for volunteers to fly six of the Avengers to Midway Island. Out of 21 pilots and aircraft there were 21 volunteers and finally the six had to be chosen by Lieutenant Langdon K. Fierberling.

Early, on the morning of 1 June 1942, the six plane detachment left Ford Island and began its eight hour, 1,300 mile flight to Midway. The Battle of Midway had yet to begin, but on landing, these six volunteers could feel the tension growing and knew that before long they would be engaging the enemy in combat.

The Avengers were prepared immediately for combat and loaded with the new torpedo that had been tested at Quonset Point. The torpedoes had been flown to Midway under the wings of PBYs. After the aircraft were readied, Lieutenant Fieberling assembled the pilots together and informed them of the eminent Japanese attack on Midway.

For the next few days there was little to do other than arise at 0400 hrs., warm up the engines of the Avengers and then remain on an alert status until 0700. The remaining hours were spent at leisure, usually exploring the small island or chasing the countless numbers of Gooney birds that inhabited the long, flat strip of land. During these idle hours, the six Avenger pilots, having noted that the other planes having wing guns usually had masking tape over the holes to keep the dust and dirt out, decided to put tape on their wings and ink in the holes where the so called guns had fired through. No reason could be explained for the action but perhaps they thought that the Japanese would believe that they carried an enormous amount of firepower.

On the morning of 4 June 1942, at approximately 0600 the six TBFs were ordered into the air. The Japanese Fleet had been sighted and was within a hundred miles of Midway. Immediately after taking off, the Avengers were to join up with Midway's Marine fighter and bomber squadrons. There was no semblance of a unified attack; just young, courageous pilots headed out to meet the onrushing Japanese. Shortly after take off, three Jap aircraft made a pass at the TBF formation but continued on their way to Midway.

Lieutenant Fieberling sighted the Japanese fleet about 0700 and began the attack immediately, under heavy attack from the enemy combat air patrol. Outnumbered three to one, the six Avengers continued their torpedo runs under the heavy fire. Several were able to release their torpedoes, scoring no hits, but before long all but one of the Avengers were completely destroyed. Five out of the original six were lost that day in the first combat performance of the TBF. It was an inauspicious beginning. The only re-

While the land based detachment of VT-8 flew the TBF into battle at Midway, their squadron mates on the Hornet met disaster in the old TBD-1. Devastators of VT-8 are shown here in February 1942 at Norfolk.

turning TBF, somehow managed to return to Midway without the aid of compass or radio which had been destroyed in the ensuing torpedo run, by the enemy aircraft. The pilot, Ensign Albert K. Earnest brought the remaining Avenger home on one main wheel and no flaps, bomb bay doors open and only limited elevator control. Along with him was H. H. Ferrier, his tunnel gunner and radio operator; the only other survivor of the Avenger detachment of Torpedo Eight. His turret gunner, J. D. Manning was killed by the Japanese combat air patrol as the attack began.

The rest of the Battle of Midway is history. The remainder of Torpedo Squadron Eight, onboard

8-T-1 the only TBF-1 to return to Midway Island after the action of 4 June 1942. Ensign Albert K. Earnest was the pilot, Aviation Machinist Mate 3rd class J. D. Manning the turret gunner and Aviation Radioman Harry H. Ferrier. Only Earnest and Ferrier survived of the 18 men from Midway based VT-8. Six TBF's took part in the battle and only 1 returned.

the HORNET, had also been completely destroyed except for one man, Ensign George Gay. On this day Torpedo Eight had lost 20 planes and 44 men, 15 TBD-1s from the HORNET and 5 TBF-1s from Midway.

The remaining portion of the Avenger detachment that had been left at Ford Island was reformed and assigned to the USS SARATOGA's (CV-3) Air Group. Under the command of Lieutanand Harold H. Larsen VT-8 found themselves engaged in battle against the Japanese in the Battle of the Eastern Solomons and the struggle for Guadalcanal. Two more Torpedo Squadrons would also be flying the new TBFs for the first time in combat. Accompanying the SARA into the Solomon Sea, were the aircraft carriers USS ENTERPRISE (CV-6) and USS WASP (CV-7). Each carried a TBF-1 squadron. VT-3 consisted of 15 Avengers and was commanded by Lieutenant Commander Charles M. Jett, while VT-7 was commanded by Lieutenant Henry A. Romberg.

These three would be the first Avenger squadrons to see action against the Japanese Fleet as complete TBF units. Their first action would be against the Japanese push for control of the Solomon Sea and the capture of the island of Guadalcanal.

On 24 August 1942, Task Force 61, which the three carriers were a part of, under the command of Vice Admiral Jack Fletcher, encountered the Japanese Fleet headed for Guadalcanal in support of its landing group. Included in the enemy striking force were the three carriers, SHOKAKU, ZUIKAKU and RYUJO.

First into battle and the first to make contact with the enemy striking force was the Air Group from ENTERPRISE. Of the seven Avengers attached to the strike group, five were able to make contact. Two were able to launch their torpedoes, no hits, and two were driven off by combat air cover. The remaining Avengers made a run at the cruiser TONE but before they could complete their attack they were driven off by fighters. One Avenger was shot down.

SARATOGA had launched her Air Group, which included 8 Avengers of VT-8 and 30 scout-bombers (SBDs) from VS-3 and VB-3. This group, having sighted the Japanese carrier RYUJO, began its attack. The SBD's screamed down from

The "Turkey" on patrol, 1942.

14,000 feet, deposited their bombs and began their retreat through heavy anti-aircraft fire and enemy fighters. The initial attack was successful as the SBDs had scored from four to ten hits. Now it was time for VT-8 to deliver the coup de grace. Lieutenant Bruce L. Herwood let the TBFs swiftly down to the smoking RYUJO, using anvil tactics, coming in from both sides of the bow so that if the enemy made a rudder shift in either direction his hull would still be exposed to the attack. The Avengers made their torpedo release at 200 feet and from less than 2,500 feet out and then concentrated on their route of escape. Only one torpedo found its target, but this, and the dive bombing attack, had sent the RYUJO to the bottom of the sea. This was the first hit that an Avenger had made on the enemy and it was made by the members of VT-8 who had lost so many of their comrades at Midway. Fortunately, not one U. S. aircraft was lost in this action.

During this action the ENTERPRISE was damaged and had to return to Pearl Harbor via Tongatabu. The carrier forces of the Japanese Navy withdrew for the time being. However, they did continue to supply their troops ashore with supplies and reinforcements, via the "Tokyo Express".

the "Toyko Express" was a thorn in the side of the Navy and Marine Corps pilots. The "Express" would enter the Guadalcanal area just before dark, making an air strike virtually impos-

VT-8 over "The Slot" off Guadalcanal, September 19

sible, deposit troops and supplies and return under the cover of darkness to the Shortland-Faisi area; out of range for the American aircraft.

On 31 August, the same day that the SARA-TOGA was hit and put out of action, the "Tokyo Express" deposited an additional 1,200 men ashore on the island.

In an effort to augment the air strength on Guadalcanal, many of the aircraft from SARA's Air Group were assigned to Henderson Field. From SARA, Guadalcanal received her first six Avengers from VT-8, under the command of Lieutenant H. H. Larsen. Additional fighters were ferried from Espiritu Santo by the WASP and HORNET on 12 September. On 15 September, when the WASP was sunk, her Air Group sent additional aircraft to Guadalcanal.

On 18 September Henderson Field added six more Avengers and 10 days later, more arrived.

At 1615, 3 October 1942, 3 Avengers participated in an attempt to stop the "Toyko Express". In a flight along with 8 SBDs commanded by Lt. (jg) F. L. Frank, one TBF managed to score a hit on a Japanese destroyer with a 500 pound bomb.

On 5 October, six Avengers from VT-8, with Lieutenant Larsen leading, made a run on the

The survivors of VT-8 at Midway meet again on Guadalcanal, October 1942. Lieutenant Albert K. Earnest is in the cockpit and Radioman Harry Ferrier is on the wing at right. Aviation Ordnanceman Rich is at left; he did not fly with VT-8 at Midway.

...y to Munda, 9 July 1943, Marine Corps TBF joins up ...amera plane and Marine photographer Bert Lynch.

TBF-1 used by Fleet Air Arm. TBF was given name of "Tarpon" by British but was later changed to "Avenger" for uniformity.

destroyer NATSUGUMO and managed to score one hit.

All through the month of October the Avengers were part of the effort to suppress the Japanese push on Henderson Field and stop the "Tokyo Express". With only one U.S. carrier, a jaunty bank of Marine and Navy aviators and a fighting bunch of Marines and soldiers, the Japanese were held in check. Finally on 26 October, the Battle of Henderson Field was over.

On 24 October, the ENTERPRISE returned to battle with the newly formed Air Group Ten. In the Air Group was one of the first Torpedo Squadrons trained in the Avenger, VT-10, commanded by Lieutenant Commander John A. Collett.

Twenty-six October found 6 of VT-10's 12 Avengers, along with 8 of VT-6s from the HORNET, engaging the Japanese Fleet. Three of the TBFs from the Big "E" were lost when jumped by Jap Zeros and the remainder were driven off before they could make an effective attack. However, the Avengers from the HORNET were able to make a torpedo run on the Japanese cruiser SUZUYA, scoring no hits. Their prey could have been larger if they had not become separated from the rest of the strike force; the SBDs from the HORNET had managed to score several hits on the Japanese carrier SHOKAKU and might have been able to finish her with the help of the Avengers. As Lieutenant Edwin B. Parker, Jr. led his 8 Avengers back to the HORNET, a second strike group was headed out and two Avengers of this group managed to make a bombing run with 500 pound bombs on the cruiser TONE, both missing.

Right side view of TBF-1

19

TBF-1 with de-icer equipment and carrying red outlined national insignia, takes to the air in June 1943.

It will have to be noted that although the Avenger and her pilots seemed to be making more misses than hits, especially on torpedo runs, their valor was highly commendable. The Avenger pilots were new to this type of warfare. Often trained in a hurry due to the need for pilots and airplanes in the South Pacific, they did one hell of a job. More often than not, they fought against heavy odds and tremendous amounts of enemy fighters and anti-aircraft fire. Also, their torpedoes were far from being absolutely effective as the United States had yet to develop a good aerial torpedo. The Japanese were far more effective because they had trained for years as torpedo pilots and had a good, dependable and effective torpedo.

The action in which the Avengers were now taking part was the famed "Battle of the Santa Cruz Islands" in which each country hurled countless aircraft into the air against one another and as at Coral Sea, a naval battle was fought without either side exchanging a shot between the surface ships.

Again the United States received the heaviest losses. HORNET was so badly damaged that she had to be abandoned and sunk by one of the U.S. destroyers. ENTERPRISE was hit, and lost the use of her forward elevator and had to return to Noumea for repairs.

At this time Roy Dahlstrom was serving onboard the HORNET and he relates this story as to the way things were.

"After the HORNET CV-8 was sunk (October 1942) Torpedo Squadron 6, consisting of 6 TBF-1s, operated off the U.S.S. NASSAU CVE-16. We had no spare parts and only the tools we had managed to steal from the ENTERPRISE CV-6.

One day, one of our TBFs flipped over on landing and broke the fuselage. I was sent ashore to make arrangements for a replacement plane and disposition of the damaged TBF-1. Since we needed spare parts, I saw the right people and was granted permission to cannabalize the damaged TBF and send it to O & R, San Diego. I came back with the good news and we stripped the plane of everything in order to support the other 5 TBFs. We were told to put the damaged Avenger on the next oil tanker that came alongside the NASSAU, to refuel her, for a trip back to the states and her eventual overhaul and repair. As we lifted the plane off the carrier, we knocked out the pins for its landing gear and they fell into the ocean. What was left of the TBF we placed on the tanker. I then made a request in the planes log book that the necessary repairs be made and I made the following notation regarding the condition of the aircraft;

JATO and the TBF. Four 330 HP jet units attached to a TBF reduced take-off runs by half the distance.

20

General Motors (Eastern Division) TBM-1 1943.

'Sorry, things are tough out here'."

Guadalcanal was now forced to fight the war without the benefit of any U.S. carrier. It was a grim situation, but somehow the Navy cruisers, destroyers and submarines, along with the aircraft stationed at Henderson Field, managed to keep the Japanese from securing a foothold either on land or sea.

The situation became critical during the month of November, and the ENTERPRISE was ordered back into action with her repairs incomplete. The forward elevator was still being repaired as she steamed into action.

Part of the ENTERPRISE's Air Group was or-dered into Henderson Field because she was unable to function at her usual pace with the still damaged elevator. Among the aircraft sent ashore were 9 TBF-1s under the command of Lieutenant John F. Sutherland. With Sutherland leading six of these, they managed to make two hits on a torpedo run against the enemy battleship HIEI on 12 November. Returning to the airfield, Sutherland had his Avengers serviced and headed back to the crippled battleship. This time he had additional support from Marine SBDs and F4Fs. The TBFs unleashed their torpedoes again; this time two bounced off the battleship's armoured sides, one ran wild,

TBF-1's in the air over California desert mid-1943.

Wake Island again forms the backdrop as TBD-1 of VT-6 pulls away from the small strip of rock and sand that made history early in WW II. Predecessor of TBF took part in raid of 24 February 1942.

VT-16 Avenger over Wake Island during raid of October 1943.

and the other two ripped into her hull with tremendous explosions. The next day HIEI's crew was removed and she sank.

On 14 November, Henderson based Avengers from the ENTERPRISE torpedoed the enemy heavy cruiser KINUSGASA, while other Avengers were making successful runs against the Japan-

ese transports attempting to bring reinforcements to Guadalcanal.

Early in November 1942, the Marine Corps Avengers arrived at Henderson Field. Lieutenant Colonel Paul Moret and his squadron, VMSB-131, a dive bombing squadron, had converted over to Avengers. After 22 days of training at Ewa they were assigned to Henderson to beef up the aerial defenses. Their squadron designation was not changed until June 1943. Four of VMSB-131's Avengers, Captain George E. Dooley, leading , had helped in the destruction of the battleship HIEI when one pilot was able to make a torpedo hit on her.

The struggle to save Guadalcanal and the effort to check the Japanese activities in the immediate area lasted on through December and into 1943. Finally on 7 February 1943, Japan evacuated the last of her troops and retreated. The United States had won and the Avengers had helped.

Following the end of the major hostilities against Guadalcanal and with a secure hold on Henderson Field, the United States now had an established foothold in the Pacific area west of Hawaii. From Henderson Field and Espiritu Santo, Marine aviators, Navy pilots and Army Air Force land based units would be able to protect Guadalcanal and continue the advance up through the Solomons. The United States Navy had been hard hit during the 'Canal' campaign and its carrier strength was low, only the SARATOGA and ENTERPRISE remained, and the new ESSEX class carriers would not be ready for action until later in the year. The USS PRINCETON CVL-23 had been launched and ready for sea

Radar equipped -3D, January 1944.

TBM-3D, January 1944.

on 25 February but would have to complete her shake down cruise, train her men and form her Air Group before moving into action against the Japanese.

The Marine Corps had added one more TBF-1 squadron and assigned them to Henderson Field. VMSB-131 had been on Guadalcanal in December of 1942 but was rotated to Espiritu Santo where they received their TBFs. Operating out of Espiritu during the early months of 1943, they later returned to Henderson Field. On returning to the U.S., VMSB-131 was redesignated VMTB-131. VMTB-143 and 144 also joined the fight in February 1943. The Marines now had three squadrons of TBF-1s stationed at Henderson.

With the Japanese being held in check throughout the Solomons during the first half of 1943 by the land based units, a new offense was being built. The Navy Department was planning a series of actions and raids that would gain the much needed islands for bases,

and isolate the Japanese forces. The plan was to become known as island-hopping. Instead of trying to push the Japanese off every island, major islands would be secured through by-passing the others and leaving many Japanese isolated without aid from the air or sea. This would split the Japanese forces and enable the United States to concentrate on major objectives.

By June 1943, the TBFs were beginning to show some promise as it was conceded that they were far superior to the Japanese torpedo plane, "Kate," in speed and endurance. Also the United States aircraft, as a whole, were starting to outclass anything the Japanese could put into the sky.

During the early months of 1943, the TBF squadrons stationed at Henderson were keeping constant pressure on the Japanese bases at Munda, Villa, Bougainville and the Shortlands.

On 20 March, 1943, 42 Marine and Navy Avengers left Henderson Field about dusk and

XTBF-3 in August 1944.

XTBF-3, 31 July 1943. This aircraft was prototype for GM built TBM-3.

headed for Kahili, 300 miles distant. This contingent, led by Major John W. Sapp of VMTB-143, each carried one, three-quarter ton, Mark-12 magnetic mine. Using Army B-17s and B-24s as a diversionary force, dropping clusters of fragmentation bombs from medium altitude, the TBFs then dropped down into the harbor and from 1,500 feet planted their mines. The diversionary tactic had worked as the airfield lit up like a Christmas tree with heavy ack-ack fire and searchlights. No TBFs were lost and the next night a second raid was carried out.

Aerial mining with the TBFs was continued and proved to be very successful at Kahili as well as other ports in the Bougainville-Shortland area. The mining missions were not without their hazards; accuracy was essential and the mines were self anchoring and had to be dropped from 800 to 1,500 feet by parachute. As the Japanese became aware of the TBF's mission they were able to pick them up with their searchlights and the casualty rate climbed.

The aerial mining was resumed in May, 1943, with over one-hundred mines being dropped in the northern Solomons area with very uncertain results. Charts and maps available at that time were very inaccurate. To the Avenger pilots it seemed that their casualties were extremely high.

On 14 February 1944, 16 TBFs of VMTB-233 attempted to mine Simpson Harbor. Only ten returned. An attempt to lay 16 mines had cost

Original XTBU-1 of 1941 still around in April 1944. Bureau Number 2542 appears on nose of aircraft.

TBM-3, November 1944.

VMTB-233 18 men and six Avengers.

On 6 July 1943, after the U.S. Fleet had stopped the "Toyko Express" from supplying its embattled garrison in Villa, ten TBFs and eleven SBDs accompanied by sixteen fighters encountered the Japanese destroyer, NAGATSUKI, and bombed her, leaving the destroyer heavily damaged, but still afloat. Later in the day, a flight of B-25s attacked the NAGATSUKI and continued the pressure, setting her magazines afire. Before dark, the magazines exploded and fire engulfed the entire ship.

All through the month of July, the Avengers continued to carry out bombing raids on the Japanese islands and made torpedo runs on Japanese shipping in Tonolei Harbor, Bougainville and the Slot.

On 19 July 1943, 6 TBFs from Henderson Field dropped one-ton bombs on two Japanese ships in the Slot. The destroyer YUGURE was sunk and the cruiser KUMANO damaged.

Although the TBF was a torpedo bomber, it was proving to be more successful as a horizontal bomber. This was due largely to the inferior torpedo that the United States was using at that time. The TBFs had been able to score several hits, but that was all. As of November 1943, a total of 26 torpedoes had been

Consolidated's TBY-2 Sea Wolf in September 1944. 1st one was delivered in November of '44, only 180 built.

launched at the Japanese and only two had been classified as effective.

On 5 November 1943, the SARATOGA and the newly arrived PRINCETON began their strikes against the Japanese stronghold of Rabaul.

The SARATOGA launched 16 Avengers and the PRINCETON 4 as a part of a massive air strike on the Japanese ships. Through heavy flack the TBFs kept their formation. As they approached the target and were parallel with it, they made quick right angle turns to launch their torpedoes.

Air Group Commander, Commander Henry H. Caldwell, flying a TBF-1C, led his strike force of SBDs and TBFs across the Crater Peninsula through a solid wall of flak in order to sweep upward and parallel to the enemy shipping. Seeking temporary refuge in a small bank of clouds, the Avengers waited until the SBDs had finished their dive bombing attack. The Avengers then made their torpedo runs, seeking out the most promising targets. The strike force left the harbor in a mass of burning flames and the retreating Avengers had to skip over and around the burning Japanese ships for four or five miles. The flames were so intense that many of the pilots doubted if they would ever make it through.

After leading the attack through the harbor and with his turret gunner wounded and radioman/photographer killed, Commander Caldwell climbed above the action to direct the remaining phases of the strike. Suddenly he found himself in the company of an F6F and 8 Zekes. Caldwell managed to drive off one of the Zekes and then returned to the SARATOGA. His safe return was

TBM-1D.

VT-7 TBM-1C grabs a wire on USS Hancock CV-19, June

nothing short of a miracle. With his Avenger shot full of holes, one wheel remaining, no flaps, no aileron, and no radio, he managed to place his airplane safely aboard the SARATOGA.

On 11 November 1943, the strike force was joined by three more carriers; the USS BUNKER HILL (CV-17), the USS ESSEX (CV-9) and the USS INDEPENDENCE (CVL-22). Their respective TBF squadrons were VT-17 (18 TBFs), VT-9 (19 TBFs) and VC-22 (9 TBFs).

With the addition of the three new carriers, an all out effort was made to destroy the Japanese fleet on the 11th. The first strike of the day was met with tremendous amounts of Japanese fighters and was not too successful. The Japanese also had put an all out attack against the U.S. carriers and the second strike was called off. The United States came out of the action with only eleven aircraft being lost, which was an astonishing feat for the amount of Japanese aircraft in the air that day.

Meanwhile the United States Marines had landed on Bougainville on 1 November 1943, and were advancing inland. Avengers were aiding in the support of the ground troops with bomb drops and strafing runs. On 14-15 December, the Marines were being hit hard from a ridge which they called "Hellzapoppin", by enemy artillery emplacements. Thirty-four Avengers of VMTB-141, each carrying 12 - 100 pound bombs with instantaneous fuses which would detonate by just hitting a tree branch, made a bombing run on the ridge. They failed to even ruffle the well dug-in Japanese. Six Avengers returned later and placed delayed action fused bombs on the Japanese position and this action ended all but token resistance.

TBM-1C's from Hancock patrol the Pacific in August 1944. Old pre-war fuselage coding was dropped as carrier moved nearer combat zone. See photo of "7-T-2."

November 1943, also found the United States starting its island hopping procedure in the Pacific. Beginning with the island of Makin and following with Tarawa, Bikini, Eniwetok and Kwajalein, the Navy was able to mass a total of eleven carriers, each equipped with Avenger squadrons, the ESSEX (CV-9), ENTER-PRISE, the new YORKTOWN (CV-10), new LEX-INGTON (CV-16), BUNKER HILL (CV-17), INDE-PENDENCE (CV-22), BELLEAU WOOD (CVL-24), COWPENS (CVL-25) and MONTEREY (CVL-26). Each TBF squadron carried the same VT number as the carrier except for SARATOGA (VT-12), YORKTOWN (VT-5), BELLEAU WOOD (VC-22B), and MONTEREY (VC-30).

The Avenger squadrons now found themselves in the role of close support for the landing forces as the United States began simultaneous attacks against Makin, Tarawa, and Betio Atoll, on 19 November.

The Japanese tried in vain to attack the United States landing forces but were driven back due to the large amount of aircraft provided by Navy and Marine squadrons. The few aircraft which they could spare was insufficient, as the majority was being used in the defense of Rabual.

On the nights of 25 and 26 November 1943, the Japanese tried to attack the United States Fleet operating off Tarawa, thus starting the Gilbert Islands action. With the aid of flares, they attempted to make torpedo runs but were unsuccessful due to some very tricky maneuvering by Rear Admiral R. K. Turner, Commander Task Force 54. As the flares were dropped by the Jap planes to illuminate the ships, he waited until the flares were halfway down and then turned his ship simultaneously, exposing only

TFB-1C of #30 Squadron, RNZAF at Whenuapai. Squadron was in transit from training at Darton Field to ops at Piva, Bougainville.

d'E. C. Darby

New Zealand TBF-1 from #30 Squadron at Espiritu Santo March 1944.

their bows. The Japanese made no bomb or torpedo hits on the night of the 25th.

On the 26th, the Japanese attempted a night attack against Admiral Radford's Carrier Group. A disastrous mistake, as Radford was the first to organize a radar-equipped, night combat air patrol. This action is said to be the first of its kind. At 1735 the first contact was made and one enemy aircraft was shot down. The combat air patrol was recalled and Admiral Radford launched the Night Fighter Group, consisting of two F6Fs and one radar-equipped Avenger. Brilliant flares lit up the sky as the Japanese torpedo planes began their runs. Lieutenant Commander John L. Phillips, an Avenger pilot, shot down the tail end torpedo bomber on radar contact. This surprised the Japanese so badly that they broke formation and started shooting at each other. No U. S. ships were hit.

By the 29th the situation was well in hand and the transports that aided in the landings, as well as the support ships not needed for the protection of the fast carriers, returned to Pearl Harbor. The Gilbert Islands action was over.

Next on the agenda was the invasion of the Marshall Islands, which included Majuro, Kawjalein, and Eniwetok.

After securing the Gilbert Islands and the surrounding areas of ocean, the carrier divisions of the Pacific Fleet were given a much needed rest, refresher training and overhauling. The land based aircraft would have to take up the slack and carry the ball for about seven weeks, until the last week of January 1944. A big help in the land based operations was that the airfield at Tarawa had become operational for fighters on 1 December 1943.

Late in January 1944, the fight for the Marshalls began and the fast carrier forces were called on to annihilate Japanese air power. The escort carriers were given the job of tactical air support of the amphibious operations, including antisubmarine patrol, strafing the landing beaches and affording close air support to the troops ashore. The fast carriers were given the task of keeping the enemy in check for protection of

Avengers on Bougainville, February 1944.

Torpedo Squadron 2 TBM-1C's from Air Group 2 on the USS Hornet CV-12, June 1944.

troop landings. Their main task was to hit the enemy on his own airfields before he could take to the air.

Throughout the Marshalls campaign, air power was used very little other than for the protection of the landing forces. For example, only 102 sorties were flown over Kwajalein on D-Day.

Early in February 1944, TBFs aided in the aerial bombardment of Eniwetok. They battered the Japanese stronghold for several days until there were very few installations visible above

the ground except for concrete blockhouses and command posts.

On 17 February, after the principal islands in the Marshalls were secured, the fast carrier force moved to strike, for the first time, against the Japanese stronghold on the island of Truk. This was the prelude to the sweep into the Marianas.

On the first night of the operations, Rear Admiral Marc A. Mitschner with Task Forces 58, launched the first night attack from the decks

Deck hands help remove wounded crewman from VT-15 TBM-1C on the USS Essex CV-9, October 1944.

TBM-1C's over the Salton Sea, California 1944. Salton Sea was one of the Navy's dive bomber ranges during the war.

of the ENTERPRISE against the Japanese shipping fleet.

Lieutenant Henry Loomis USNR, the radar expert who had started the radar school at Pearl Harbor, and Lieutenant William L. Martin, a specialist in night flying, had pioneered the methods of night flying with radar. They found that by careful instrument flying with the use of radar, one could approach within a few hundred yards of a beach on the darkest of nights. They had borrowed TBFs while stationed at Pearl Harbor and tested their theories bombing the reefs around the island of Espiritu Santo. Torpedo Squadron Ten, aboard the ENTERPRISE, was given specially equipped Avengers (TBF-1Cs) for night bombing tactics. Shortly before the strike against Truk, Martin was promoted to Lieutenant Commander, and given the command of VT-10.

While operating under darkness 100 miles off Truk, the attack group consisting of 12 TBF-1Cs, was launched at 0200 under overcast skies. Each carried four, 500-pound general-purpose bombs. Rendezvousing over the target, with the aid of Aldis lamps and running lights, the Avengers began their attack. After locating the enemy ships in the harbor by radar, the Avengers began to make deliberate runs at masthead height at a speed of 180 knots, spaced at one-minute intervals. The anti-aircraft fire was intense, but not accurate, except when the planes' exhausts were sighted. A total of 25 runs was made which resulted in 13 direct hits, 7 near misses, and two hits on islets mistaken for enemy ships. This night bombing run resulted in about one-third of the total damage inflicted on the enemy

shipping at Truk. The only sad note of the whole operation was that Lieutenant Commander Martin, who had originated night bombing raids, did not lead the strike because of an accident. The strike was led by the squadrons Executive Officer, Lieutenant E. Van Eason, with Lieutenant William B. Chance as radar operator.

The next morning, 18 February 1944, full-scale operations were resumed against Truk by the ENTERPRISE, YORKTOWN, ESSEX, and BUNKER HILL. The harbor was almost clear of any live targets and the strike force began to pay special attention to airfields, storage tanks, hangars, and ammunition dumps. By noon, Admiral Mitscher recalled the attack forces. The combined Air Groups had flown 1,250 combat sorties, dropped 400 tons of torpedoes and bombs on Japanese shipping, and 94 tons of bombs on airfields and shore installations.

The two day strike had left devastating results. A total of 29 ships had been sunk or left in an inoperable state. Five Avenger pilots from the ENTERPRISE, led by Lieutenant Grady Owens, made a well timed attack on the Japanese destroyer FUMIZUKI, steaming to sea at 27 knots. The coordinated attack lasted only 90 seconds, and only one torpedo hit was recorded.

The combined Air Groups had also left the Japanese without the use of approximately 275 aircraft. The strike was the most successful carrier operation of the war up to that time and enabled the capture of Eniwetok to proceed without any interference from the Japanese air forces.

March 1944, found the fast carrier striking force of the ENTERPRISE, BUNKER HILL and

Avengers from Marine training group, 27 October 1944.

HORNET hitting the Japanese shipping and airfields of Palau. The fighter squadrons of the respective Air Groups spent the first few days of the action strafing and bombing the enemy shipping and shore lines. Specially equipped Avengers were used to mine the harbor and seal up Japanese shipping. As the TBFs began their mining runs, 24 Japanese vessels were situated in the harbor. Eight were underway in an attempt to break out but turned back. The destroyer, WAKATAKE, and repair ship, AKASHI, were at sea. Torpedo bearing Avengers made a run on the WAKATAKE and sent her to the bottom. The AKASHI was left to the divebombers, which destroyed her.

The mine laying Avengers were able to seal up the harbor and the 32 ships that were contained were left to the mercy of the Air Groups.

Coordinated strikes were also carried out against the Japanese held islands of Hollandia and Truk. Japanese air strikes were few and those that did venture forth usually met with destruction. The Avengers were now assisting in close ground support for landings throughout the area as the United States began an all out drive on Biak, Hollandia, New Guinea, Noemfoor, and Sansapor.

Early in June 1944, the fast carrier force moved into the Marianas area with a total of 15 carriers, divided into four groups. Under the command of Admiral Mitscher the four groups consisted of HORNET, (CV-12), YORKTOWN (CV-10), BELLEAU WOOD (CVL-24), and BATAAN (CVL-29), BUNKER HILL (CV-17); WASP CV-18); MONTEREY (CVL-26); and CABOT (CVL-28); ENTERPRISE (CV-6); LEXINGTON (CV-16); PRINCETON (CVL-23) and SAN JACINTO (CVL-30);

ESSEX (CV-9); LANGLEY (CVL-27); and COWPENS (CVL-25).

The carriers first neutralized the Japanese airfields at Yap, Peleliu, Woleai, and Truk. Then the four groups headed for the islands of Guam, Tinian and Saipan to aid in the landings and capture of these enemy strongholds.

On 13 June 1944, a number of the LEXINGTON'S Avengers were armed with rockets. Although rocket attacks had been used by the Royal Air Force for a year or so, this was a new form of armament for the U.S. Pacific Fleet. The rocket laden Avengers led by Lieutenant Commander Robert E. Isely, squadron commander, made their runs against the Japanese airfield, Aslito Field, in shallow glides, launching rockets at 1,000 to 2,000 yards. Isely's Avenger and two others were hit by anti-aircraft fire during the glides. Isely's and one other Avenger burst into flames and crashed. Two entire crews were killed. Isely was one of the Navy's most distinguished pilots and after a brilliant performance in the hunter-killer groups in the Atlantic, had been transferred to the Pacific. This loss convinced the air officers of the carriers that rocket launching, unless at close range, was out of the question for the TBF. However, the air strikes continued against the Japanese held islands as the TBFs dropped a countless number of general purpose bombs on shore installations and airfields.

Saipan was invaded on 15 June and 72 aircraft from the escort carriers, including 12 Avengers armed with rockets, made low level runs on the beaches and the area just beyond in support of the amphtracts carrying the assault troops.

The fast carriers were now moving throughout

Power operated ball turret and caliber 50 machine gun gave TBF good protection from the rear.   *T. E. Doll*

Torpedo bay of Avenger could carry varied load of destruction.   *T. E. Doll*

the Pacific with little or no resistance from the Japanese air forces. With control of the skies, the carriers were able to offer almost their entire Air Groups for close air support of the invasion forces. During June and July of 1944 the United States was able to gain control of Tinian, Saipan and Guam.

However, one of the most historical battles was taking place during the same period of time. The Battle of the Philippine Sea was in full swing and the largest aerial battle ever staged between two opposing carrier forces was shaping up. This was to become known as the "Marianas Turkey Shoot." *

The first day of the battle, 19 June, belonged to the F6F Hellcats as the Japanese carriers launched four separate air strikes against the United States Fleet. Each time, the combat air patrols met the Japanese aircraft and sent them crashing into the sea. The Japanese also sent out a striking force from Orate Field, Guam, but the United States carrier forces were able to repel the strike before it could assemble and head for the U.S. carrier forces. In the ensuing battle, Orate was destroyed and every attack that the Japanese sent out met with almost total destruction. During the first day the Japanese lost approximately 156 airplanes trying to get at the fast carrier force.

The next day, 20 June, Lieutenant R. S. Nelson, USNR, flying in an Avenger from the ENTERPRISE, made the first contact by a carrier pilot of the Japanese Fleet. In all the days of fighting in and around the islands in the Philippine Sea, he was the first to sight an enemy combat ship.

The time was late, 1540, and Mitscher, knowing that only a few hours of daylight were left, ordered his carriers to launch a strike. From the

* S. E. Morrison, Vol. 8, pg. 275. Cdr. Paul D. Buie of VF-16 in LEXINGTON, who liked to compare the downing of enemy planes with shooting wild turkey, was responsible for the name.

HORNET, BUNKER HILL, YORKTOWN, WASP, ENTERPRISE, LEXINGTON, BELLEAU WOOD, BATAAN, MONTEREY, CABOT and SAN JACINTO, 85 fighters, 77 dive-bombers and 54 Avengers were launched. Each knew, as did Mitscher, that the odds of hitting the Japanese Fleet and returning before dark was almost impossible. Still, they went. They knew that the Japanese would not be expecting them under these conditions.

Four Avengers from the BELLEAU WOOD, led by Lieutenant (jg) Brown, made a torpedo run on the enemy carrier HIYO. Brown had vowed to torpedo a Japanese carrier at any cost. Leading his four Avengers through heavy flack, his port wing was shot away; fire erupted filling the center section of the plane with flames which forced his radioman and gunner to bail out. Now alone in the Avenger, Brown continued the attack and on the way in, the fire burned itself out. He released his torpedo, hitting the HIYO. Browns wingman, Lieutenant (jg) Benjamin C. Tate USNR, launched his torpedo and missed. However, a third torpedo, dropped by Lieutenant (jg) Omark found its mark and exploded.

Tate and Omark, after eluding several Japanese planes, found Brown and his badly shot up Avenger and tried to lead him out of the battle area. Brown, wounded badly and unable to steer his aircraft, disappeared into a cloud and was lost.

Lieutenant Van Eason and five Avengers from the ENTERPRISE carrying bombs, managed to score a few hits on the carrier RYUHO, but were unable to sink her.

The Avengers, bomb loaded, also made a dive-bombing attack on SUIKAKU, but were unable to sink her although several hits were reported. Both of these enemy carriers were able to escape and return home for repairs. Had the Avengers been carrying torpedoes, the story

VT-83 TBM-3 shortly before carrier air group markings were abandoned in favor of standardized carrier ID symbols. Escorting F4U's are from Marine Corps VMF-124, 1st. USMC squadron to serve on the big Essex class carriers. January 1945. Carrier is Essex CV-9.

might have been different.

As the Japanese fleet retired from battle, the two day fight had cost him dearly. Out of 430 airplanes that were in his hangars and on his flight decks, only 35 were operational. He also lost two of his carriers, SHOKAKU and TAIHO to the U.S. submarine Albacore.

Mitscher's fighting and courageous pilots began to head for home as the battle ended at 1900. Darkness was setting in, gas was low and there were dim hopes of being able to find the carrier force in the darkness, let alone make a night landing. Every man knew that his chances were slim, as they were at war and the Task Force would be blacked out and silent as a precaution against enemy submarines that might be in the area. Every pilot nursed his almost dry gas tank in an all out effort to return.

Onboard the LEXINGTON, Admiral Mitscher knew that the situation was critical; by turning on the lights of the Fleet to aid the pilots he would be risking the entire force. However, there were many men in those returning aircraft that were in their early twenties; some not old enough to vote. They were tired, almost out of gas and had little experience in night landings. The decision was a tough one. Below deck a sailor wrote on a small piece of paper:

* "The friendly chickens are staggering back,

Make, O'Lord, thy night less black,

For the friendly chickens are having hard

flying,

And some of our boys are dying."

*"THE END OF AN EMPIRE" by Captain Walter Karig, USNR. From a poem on page 250 written by an unknown sailor aboard the USS LEXINGTON (CV-16) Published by Holt, Rinehart and Winston Inc.

In the radio rooms throughout the Fleet the voices of the pilots could be heard as they asked for a fix as to their position. Then admiral Mitscher made the only decision he could have made. He ordered all the lights turned on. Not just the deck lights, but the flood lights and the searchlights as well. Many of the pilots were able to make it to their respective carriers. Some landed on different carriers. Many, low on fuel, were unable to even make an approach and ditched their airplanes into the sea; but at least they now had a chance to be picked up by the many destroyers in the area.

In the final analysis, obtained sometime after the war, the Japanese had lost 243 aircraft in its effort to sink the fast carrier force of the United States Navy. In addition, 22 aircraft were lost when the TAIHO and the SHOKAKU went down. Many of these two ships' aircraft were sent to Guam and of course were also lost in the air strikes there. Many of the Japanese aircraft were destroyed on the ground and the final total was 476.

The U.S. losses were 130 aircraft, 33 crewmen and 16 pilots. The majority of the aircraft were lost as the pilots attempted to land on the carriers, that last night.

The Marine Corps Avenger squadrons were also beginning to see more action as the United States began securing more and more islands and establishing airfields from whence they could strike. VMTB-131 was the first Marine Avenger squadron to operate from Guam. They landed on 11 August 1944, under the command of Major George E. Dooley. Major W. W. Dean and

CAPTION FOR OPPOSITE PAGE:
"TBM-3 Avenger of VMTB-132 prepares for strike against Japanese on deck of USS CAPE GLOUCESTER CVE-109.

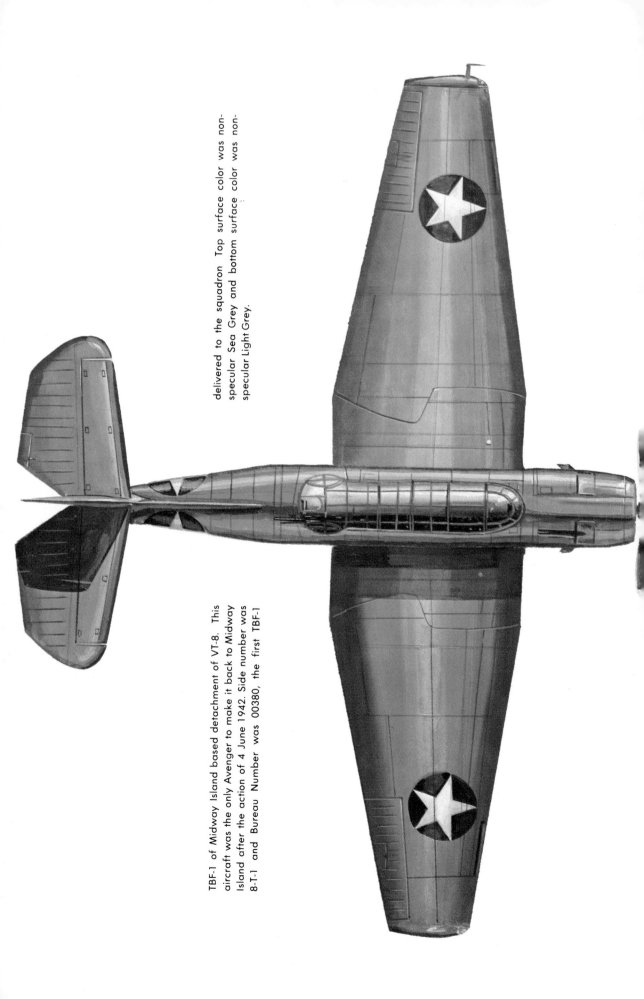

TBF-1 of Midway Island based detachment of VT-8. This aircraft was the only Avenger to make it back to Midway Island after the action of 4 June 1942. Side number was 8-T-1 and Bureau Number was 00380, the first TBF-1 delivered to the squadron. Top surface color was non-specular Sea Grey and bottom surface color was non-specular Light Grey.

Scale 1:72

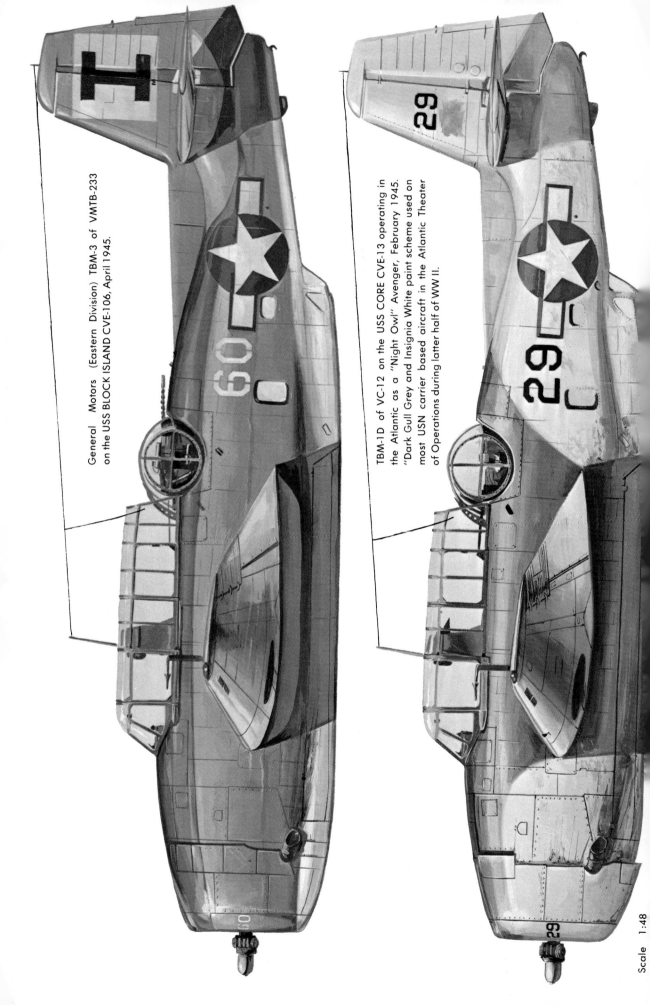

General Motors (Eastern Division) TBM-3 of VMTB-233 on the USS BLOCK ISLAND CVE-106, April 1945.

TBM-1D of VC-12 on the USS CORE CVE-13 operating in the Atlantic as a "Night Owl" Avenger, February 1945. "Dark Gull Grey and Insignia White paint scheme used on most USN carrier based aircraft in the Atlantic Theater of Operations during latter half of WW II.

Scale 1:48

VMTB-233 TBM-3 on the deck of the first all-Marine carrier the USS Block Island CVE-106, 7 February 1945.

his Avenger squadron, VMTB-242, reported to the newly won island of Tinian. Both squadrons were assigned to anti-submarine patrol duties. VMTB-134 arrived on the island of Peleiu in October 1944, and aided the ground forces with close air support in the mopping-up operations. As the fast carrier forces of the Fleet began to sweep island after island, additional Marine Avenger squadrons were placed on the captured real estate.

The fast carrier forces began their final push against the Japanese as they headed for the islands of Okinawa, Formosa and Leyte. From 10

October to 14 October, Avenger squadrons operating from the carriers took part in air strikes against Formosa. Seeking out enemy shipping and airfields the Navy squadrons were able to destroy 500 enemy aircraft, about 20 freighters, numerous small craft, and an enormous amount of ammunition dumps, hangars, barracks, and industrial plants.

Several strikes were also carried out against the Japanese stronghold of Okinawa as the battle began to take the form of carrier based aircraft against land based aircraft.

On 17 October 1944, Admiral Halsey began to

TBM-3's on patrol.

Marine Corps TBM-3 waits on Iwo Jima's Motoyama Airstrip #2 while R4D makes landing, March 1945. Squadron is VMTB-242.

VMTB-242 TBM-3 prepares for take off from Iwo Jima for anti-sub patrol around the island, March 1945.

move his Fast Carrier Forces into position to strike against Luzons' airfields and enemy shipping in Manila Bay.

The main landings commenced on 20 October at Tacloban, capital of Leyte, and at Dulag. During the first four days, Avengers from two of the escort carrier groups supported the ground forces ashore while the third group concentrated on the Japanese airfields on Cebu, Negros, Pauay, Bohol and Northern Mindanao. Principal targets were Japanese aircraft, since their destruction became more important than damaging the airfields which were far too numerous. During the first three days of action the escort carriers destroyed 125 aircraft.

The 26th TBF-1 delivered to the Navy in January, 1942, was still going strong in the summer of 1944. She was on her third set of log books and her fifth or sixth engine. She was shot up and battered, but old 26 was still in the service of the Navy, hauling spare parts and towing targets, still reliable, still on duty.

On 24 October the Japanese made contact with the Fast Carrier Force as they attempted to stop its advance through the Pacific Islands.

Before Admiral Halsey could issue his strike order, Japanese naval aircraft from Luzon were beginning to make their attacks on the Fleet. One Betty was able to make a bomb hit on the PRINCETON, causing a tremendous explosion

three decks below and igniting several Avengers. The PRINCETON stopped, dead in the water. Fires quickly spread throughout the ship and although the PRINCETON was still seaworthy, no other ship was available to take her in tow. Due to the extensive fires onboard the PRINCETON, she was abandoned and was torpedoed by two U.S. destroyers.

Meanwhile, fighters, bombers and Avengers from the INTREPID, CABOT, LEXINGTON and ESSEX attacked the Japanese Fleet. Avengers from the CABOT and INTREPID were able to make eight torpedo hits on the battleship MUSASHI. The FRANKLIN and ENTERPRISES' Avengers added ten more torpedoes to the number and the big battleship was left to flounder in the sea, finally sinking.

At the same time the Escort Carriers, which had been divided into three forces known as Taffy 1, Taffy 2 and Taffy 3, were engaged by a large Japanese attack force. This was the first time that the Escort Carriers had operated without the larger carriers in an action. Taffy 1 was the first of the United States force to receive the famed Japanese Kamikaze attacks.

Into the Leyte operations came the USS INDEPENDENCE with the first Night Air Group of the War. Designated Night Air Group 41, the INDEPENDENCE carried two squadrons. VFN-41 and 3 F6F-3s, 2 F6F-5s and 14 F6F-5Ns and under

Dust on Iwo's Motoyama Airstrip #1 all but hides this TBM-3 from the USS Hoggatt Bay CVE-75, March 1945.

-2 in the air during 1944. Glossy Sea Blue paint adorns somewhat "slimmed down" twin to the Avenger.

Hancock's VT-6 TBM-3 on deck, April 1945. Curtiss SB2C's of VB-6 await take off.

the command of Commander T. F. Caldwell (also Air Group Cdr.), and VTN-41 with 8 TBM-1Ds under the command of Lt. W. R. Taylor USNR. The INDEPENDENCE gave the U.S. Fleet much needed night protection and also conducted night raids against the islands.

The next day, 25 October, Admiral Mitscher on the LEXINGTON and commanding Task Force 38, entered into the "Battle of Cape Engano". Launching his Air Groups even before an actual "contact" confirmation from his scouts, the pilots began a sweep of the area. At 0800 contact with the Japanese Fleet was established and they began making their runs on the Japanese ships. The Helldivers began with bomb strikes, followed by the Avengers with torpedo strikes.

With Commander David McCampbell, Air Group 15 commander from the ESSEX, acting as target coordinator, the first strike force was able to administer a small amount of damage on the Japanese ships. As the first strike force regrouped for its return to the carriers, a second strike was already under way. In all, Commander McCampbell directed a total of five strike forces against the Japanese Fleet, each time guiding the pilots to the most opportune targets.

The total amount of damage was not estimated to an accurate degree but the battle was later to prove rather decisive. Many of the Japanese ships were badly damaged and would never again become fully operational. The Avengers were able to make several torpedo hits and every Carrier Air Group had claimed some sort of damage inflicted. Torpedo and bomber pilots were finding it easier to make their runs as the Japanese air cover was almost non-existant.

From 12 November to 25 November, the Fast Carrier Force continued to hit the Japanese held islands; this time concentrating on the island of Luzon. The Avengers helped destroy the Japanese ships in the harbors and the airfield installations throughout the island. Avenger operations were becoming more routine as each Japanese island was captured, and new airfields were established for the United States forces. From Luzon to Mindoro and Mindanao, the liberation of the Philippines found the Avenger squadrons in constant use.

On 28 December, the USS ENTERPRISE, newly converted into a night carrier, joined the INDEPENDENCE and a new night-flying carrier task group was formed. The ENTERPRISE Night Air Group was commanded by Commander W.

TBM-3's of VMTB-232 "The Red Devils," over Okinawa, April 1945.

USS Antietam CV-36 TBM-3's over coast of China, 1945. VT-89 is the squadron.

I. Martin, pioneer of night flying tactics. Under Martin's command were VFN-90 flying F6F-5Ns, -5Fs and 5Ps and VTN-90 outfitted with TBM-3Ds. During the final stages of the war. Martin was flying his Avenger over the mainland of Japan on the night of 12 April 1945; his radar-man was Lieutenant W. B. Chace. While heading for the target area his Avenger was picked up by a large number of searchlight beams. Quick to rise to the occasion, Martin began releasing small pieces of tinfoil which caused the Japanese radar system to malfunction. The searchlights began skirting over the sky, utterly confused with the free floating tinfoil. Martin then proceeded to wing his Avenger over and made continued rocket attacks on the searchlight positions.

Through December 1944 and into January 1945, the Carrier Force continued to sweep deeper into Japanese waters. In January 1945, Admiral Halsey achieved his long desired quest as he entered into the South China Sea.

The Fast Carrier Force, spearheaded by the ENTERPRISE and the INDEPENDENCE and designated Task Group 38.5, and under the command of Admiral M. B. Gardner, began a search sweep for Japanese ships on 12 January. On 16 January, the night-flying Avengers carried out strikes against Japanese weather stations and shipping on the China Coast and Formosa. However, due to the low overcast, most of the attacks

Mail plane prepares to take off from Nan Yuan Airfield, Peiping, China, operating base of Marine Air Group 24 on daily run to Tientsin. Late 1945.

were not too successful; although several destroyers and freighters were damaged. The Task Groups remained in the South China Sea from 10 January to 20 January and covered 3,800 miles.

From 19 February to 10 March the Avengers were involved in the Iwo Jima campaigns; mostly in the role as close air support aircraft covering the landings and helping to soften up the Japanese installations; and in April their efforts were turned to Okinawa.

One of the last major battles that the Avengers fought as torpedo bombers was in the sinking of the famed Japanese battleship, YAMATO. The YAMATO was the pride of the Japanese Navy and the worlds largest battleship.

The YAMATO, moving toward Okinawa in support of its besieged troops, was first sighted at 0820 on 7 April by an airplane from the USS ESSEX. Two pilots from VPB-21, Lieutenant James R. Young USNR, and Lieutenant (jg) R. L. Simms flying PBM-3s, spotted the ship shortly thereafter, and shadowed it for the next five hours.

Admiral Mitscher, as soon as he received contact reports, launched a tracking and covering group of 16 fighters at 0915. At 1000 Task Group 58.1 and 58.3 began launching aircraft which consisted of 280 airplanes, 98 of them Avengers.

At 1241 the YAMATO received the first strike as two 500 pound bombs found their mark and four minutes later the first torpedo made its

VT-28 TBM-1C's in the air July 1945. Tail letter "C" replaced Monterey's geometric ID symbol in July of that year.

way through the water and exploded in her forward section. The hit was assumed to be delivered by an Avenger from the USS BENNINGTON, VT-82. Aircraft from the SAN JACINTO managed one bomb hit on the destroyer HANAKAZE. The HANAKAZE also received one torpedo hit in the bow from an Avenger attached to VT-45. The HANAKAZE went to the bottom. The light cruiser YAHAGI was also hit by a torpedo and went dead in the water. From 1337 to 1417 YAMATO and her supporting force were under almost continuous attack. Avengers were able to place five more torpedos in her port side, creating serious flooding and fires. With only one screw working and listing badly, YAMATO lost speed rapidly. Another attack by the Avengers was successful as several more torpedoes found their mark, splitting her sides.

TBM's from the USS Monterey CVL-26 in the air, August 1945.

Marine TBM's from Ewa are in the air to participate in Honolulu's VJ Day parade. 3 September 1945. Ewa planes carried letters "V" or "W" on fuselage for ID purposes.

Ten more bombs, several from Avengers, also found their mark. At 1400 the final attack allowed the Avengers and Hellcats to make selective runs on the Japanese giant. Several more torpedoes ripped into her sides and at 1423 the YAMATO slipped beneath the sea to her watery grave.

One Avenger pilot, Lieutenant (jg) W. E. Delaney from the BELLEAU WOOD, had a grandstand seat for the final moments of the YAMATO. His Avenger had made several bomb runs on the YAMATO, scoring several hits. However, one of his runs was at such a low altitude that the explosion of his bomb ignited his airplane and he and his crew had to bail out. The two crewmen were lost but Delaney managed to inflate his life raft and escape. Climbing aboard his raft he was able to witness the death of the YAMATO.

Lieutenant Young and Lieutenant (jg) Simms, who had been tracking the YAMATO during the battle, spotted the downed aviator. While Simms used his PBM as a decoy to draw the enemy fire, Young made a water landing, picked up Delaney, and then made a jet-assisted take off. Young then returned Delaney to Yontan airfield.

At 1701 Admiral Mitscher sent his final message of the battle to Admiral Spruance. The report had declared the final tally to stand as the YAMATO, AGANO and YAHAGI sunk (one battleship, two light cruisers), seven or eight destroyers also sunk, two left burning rather badly and three escaped. The Fast Carrier Force lost seven planes.

The remainder of the War is history. Okinawa was secured in July and the Japanese surrendered on 15 August 1945.

The Avengers and the men who flew them had come a long way since the Battle of Midway in 1942. The Avenger had been battered and bruised and pushed around by a much superior force during the early days of the war, but the pilots who flew her had pride in her and grew to respect her as a close and warm friend. The Japanese, in the early days, were better torpedo bomber pilots since they had years of experience and were trained just for that job. Avenger pilots in the early days had made very few torpedo drops and were inexperienced. Basically, the Avenger failed in her task from the Midway Battle into early 1943. As the pilots gained experience they were more able to use the Avenger for the role for which she was designed. In the Battle of the Phillipines, the Avenger once again proved that she could deliver a torpedo to a target with good results. Once again in the sinking of the YAMATO, the Avengers delivered the hardest blows, from torpedoes as well as bombs. Every action that the Avenger participated in was successful and she remained as an aircraft to the Fleet until 1955.

In the words of the late Grant Daley, "The Avenger was a good airplane."

USS Santee CVE-29 TBM's taxi under direction of Japanese plane director on Formosa's Matsuyama Airfield. Carrier planes were bringing in supplies for American POW's after fall of Japan. September 1945.

Chapter 3

THE ATLANTIC

Only TBF-1 carried by the Ranger during Operation Torch, was flown by Commander D. B. Overfield, CAG-9.

It may seem strange that an airplane primarily designed as a torpedo bomber would find its greatest claim to fame as a depth charging, sub killing machine in a theater of war that gave most of the headlines to the great air and land battles that raged over and on the continent of Europe. Carrier based naval air in the Atlantic had its own unique style; that being anti-submarine warfare. Operation Torch, the invasion of French North Africa, proved an exception to this rule and provided naval air with its first of two opportunities to participate in a full scale amphibious landing in the European Theater.

On 9 November 1942, planes from four US

TBF-1's, F4F-4's and SBD-3's on Ranger during Operation Torch. Avengers are believed to be from other carrier as Ranger does not list TBF's on her roster at this time.

A TBF-1C of VC-55 from the USS Card CVE-13, floats in the green waters of the Atlantic after mishap in January 1943.

carriers took to the air in support of this landing; they were: USS SANGAMON (ACV-26)* with VGS-26 aboard - 9 TBF-1's; 9 SBD-3's; VGF-26 - 12 F4F-4's. USS SUWANEE (ACV-27) with VGS-27 aboard - 9 TBF-1's; VGS-30 - 6 F4F-4's, VFG-27 - 11 F4F-4's; VGF-28 - 12 F4F's. USS SANTEE (ACV-29) with VGS-29 aboard - 8 TBF-1's; 9 SBD-3's; VGF-29 - 12 F4F-4's. USS RANGER** (CV-4) with Air Group 9 aboard - VF-9 - 27 F4F-4's; VF-41 - 27 F4F-4's; VS-41 - 18 SBD-3's.

Avenger air action during Torch consisted mainly of bombing and strafing runs against the Vichy French but on one occasion she proved to be fairly proficient at tank busting.

*ACV (Auxiliary Aircraft Carrier) later changed to CVE (Escort Aircraft Carrier).

**RANGER operated only 1 TBF; it belonged to CDR. D. B. Overfield, Commander of Air Group 9.

German submarine U-185 is attacked and damaged by planes of USS Core CVE-13, 23 August 1943.

Lieutenant R. Y. McElroy of VGS-26 was flying a routine patrol in search of targets of opportunity when he came upon a number of enemy tanks which, upon spotting his TBF, quickly headed into a Eucalyptus grove for protection. McElroy pursued the tanks as they dashed for cover and flew so low during his attack that upon returning to the Sangamon to refuel and rearm, the smell of Eucalyptus oil could be detected on the leading edges of his wings. After replenishing his fuel and ammunition he took to the air, located the tanks again and supervised an aerial attack that routed and scattered them in all directions. One tank was assumed destroyed with minor damage to the rest. McElroy's TBF received a total of 13 hits during this engagement.

Missions flown and losses of USN aircraft for

VC-13 TBF's blast U-185 and send it to bottom of Atlantic in August 1943.

44

TBM-1 being launched from deck of USS Kasaan Bay CVE-69, February 1944. Kasaan Bay took part in the Invasion of So. France later in year. Operation Dragon, July 1944.

the period of 8 to 11 November 1942 are as follows: Santee - 144 missions - 21 planes lost, 7 of these were TBF-1's. Suwannee - 255 missions - 5 planes lost, 2 of these were TBF-1's. Sangamon - 183 missions - 3 planes lost, 1 of them a TBF-1.

In March of 1943, the first escort carrier group for convoy support was built around the USS BOGUE CVE-9. She carried the 12 F4F-4 Wildcats and 8 TBF-1's of VC (Composite Squadron) -9. Bogue's first 2 convoys turned up only 2 sub

sightings with no sinkings. However on 21 May, VC-9's skipper, LCdr. Drane, attacked U-231 and damaged it enough that the U Boat had to withdraw from her patrol and retire for repairs. LCdr. Drane flew a TBF-1. On 22 May, the submarine U-569 was destroyed by 2 TBF's from Bogue flown by Lt. (jg) W. F. Chamberlain and Lt. H. S. Roberts.

Avengers operating in the Atlantic normally carried 4 depth charges and made low angle

Composite Squadron 8 TBM-3 is prepared for launch from deck of USS Mission Bay CVE-59 in December 1943.

Plenty of action on the deck of the USS Charger CVE-30 in December 1943.

approaches toward the target. They had the speed to make their runs and bomb the submarine before it could complete its dive and because of this speed the TBF could retire quickly beyond anti-aircraft range.

In June of 1943, a U.S. Navy pilot in an Avenger was credited with saving an Africa bound convoy of LST's from submarine attack by forcing U-603 to submerge and retire from the area by dropping 3 of his depth charges. The TBF was proving itself in both the Atlantic and Pacific with the best scores yet to come.

In mid-1943, the CVE air groups began teaming the F4F Wildcat and TBF together into Hunter/ Killer groups with great success. On 5 June 1943, an F4 and TBF from Bogue's VC-9 made a combined attack on U-217, then 63 miles from Bogue. The F4 made 3 strafing runs on the sub, killing several gunners and starting a fire in the conning tower, then the TBF dropped her depth charges from approximately 100' with devastating effects. The U Boat plunged and was not seen again.

Mid 1943 also saw the introduction of the new homing torpedo called Fido, this new weapon

TBM-1 of VC-6 from the USS Tripoli CVE-64, August 1944. Tripoli operated in the Atlantic at this time.

3 tone grey paint scheme adorns TBF on deck of USS Randolph CV-15 during the carrier's shakedown cruise in the Atlantic, November 1944.

made the Hunter/Killer team more effective than ever before.

The Wildcat would force the enemy submarine to dive, then the TBF would drop the Fido which quickly found the sub and either completely destroyed it or caused heavy damage.

The Atlantic Hunter/Killer teams did enjoy great success but they did suffer losses from time to time. On 8 August 1943, a team from the USS CARD CVE-11, took on U-664 and U-262; both subs were looking for a fight, and luck, it turned out, was on their side. Both U-664 and 262 scored

several hits on the TBF which forced it to ditch. The F4 ran into heavy fire from U-262 and was shot down, its pilot lost.

By 1944, the Nazi submarines began surfacing only at night to take on fuel and recharge their batteries. The CVE air groups did a good job in keeping the submarines down all day but this kept the number of "kills" at a standstill. To effectively engage the U Boats would mean that night air operations would have to be initiated and at the time carrier air ops was still a daylight hours activity, save for a few specially trained in-

TBM-1D "Night Owl" avenger from the USS Core CVE-13, February 1945. Squadron is VC-12. "Night Owl" TBM's had all guns removed and replaced by extra gas tanks enabling the aircraft to stay on station for as much as 14 hours. They acted as the eyes of the night flying Hunter - Killer groups in the North Atlantic in the latter half of WW II.

TBM-3 of VC-19 lines up for launch from BOGUE CVE-9 in April 1945. Rocket launchers and low-viz Atlantic Theater paint scheme are shown to advantage in this excellent USN photograph. Photo credit — USN

dividuals. Some TBF's were being outfitted as night flying planes, their bombs and turret guns were removed and replaced with fuel tanks that enabled the TBF to stay in the air up to 14 hours. These special TBF's became known as "Nightowls," but still the problem of night ops was not solved.

By April of 1944, night flying, take offs and landing from a carrier deck finally became a reality. After a few bad experiences in the early stages of the night operations game, Captain Dan Gallery, skipper of the USS GUADALCANAL CVE-60, VC-58 CO LCdr. Dick Gould and the little CVE's LSO (Landing Signal Officer) Lt. Jarvis Jennings together with a "little bit of luck", made it work. One can imagine how difficult it must be trying to land a TBF on the short 512' flight deck of a Kaiser Class carrier during the day but a landing at night must have appeared almost impossible at first. The night operations, pioneered by Captain Gallery's pilots, both VC-58 and VC-8, won the argument for night ops in the Atlantic and from mid-1944 to VE Day, night ops became standard procedure aboard the CVE's in the Atlantic.

By the end of 1944 around the clock operations against the Germans were in full swing; a total of 48 U Boats had been destroyed by the small CVE air groups from May 1943 until the end of 1944. By May 1945, a grand total of 53 German submarines would be credited to the carrier air groups. The TBF/TBM Avenger took the "Lion's Share" of accolades in this action. It was the Avenger that carried the depth charges and Fidoes that spelled the end to the Nazi submarine threat in the Atlantic.

★ ★ ★ ★ ★ ★ ★ ★ ★

Chapter 4

WEEKEND WARRIORS
AND THE TBM

NAS Willow Grove, Pennsylvania Reserve TBM-3W, 1949.   *Photo credit — Brian Baker.*

Beautiful study of TBM-3U in flight, 1948.
Photo credit — USN via Larkins

With the coming of peace in 1945, the United States Navy started the great de-mobilization of men and aircraft. Many of the latest aircraft in its inventory, some of which had never fired a shot in anger, were "mothballed" and shipped out to lonely Arizona deserts. These were the more fortunate ones, as many were routed to the scrap yards and ended up as pots and pans in miladys kitchens.

The Navy, always looking ahead, took positive

Avenger in utility markings; fuselage is glossy sea blue; wings are orange-yellow with insignia red stripes; horizontal stabilizer and vertical fin is orange-yellow with insignia red rudder.
Photo credit — USN via Larkins

TBM-3's, Okinawa based, HEDRON 14, USMC, 1947-48.

strides to make sure that they would always have a reserve aviation force to call on in the event that another national emergency should arise.

On 1 July 1946, the Naval Air Reserve Training Command was established with Headquarters located at the Naval Air Station, Glenview, Illi-

Bottom view of TBM-3.

TBM-3E's in flight 1948.

nois. Within two years the Command had established stations in 28 cities throughout the continental United States. Included in the command were torpedo squadrons operating in TBM-3E's.

The Avengers became a familiar sight during the early post World War II years. Along with other Naval World War II aircraft; Vought F4U Corsairs, Curtiss SB2C Helldivers and Grumman

Utility TBM-3, 1950.

TBM-3S and TBM-3W being readied for launch from the USS Palau CVE-122, June 1951.
Photo credit - Bill Balough.

F6F Hellcats, the Avengers filled the Saturday and Sunday skies over the sleepy mid-western sections of the United States and busy cities on the East and West coasts. These aircraft, flown by Naval Reservists, better known as Weekend Warriors, became the backbone for many experimental ideas in the advancement of Anti-submarine Warfare. Using techniques developed by the

Early TBM-3W.   *Photo credit — Grumman*

Intended to replace the TBF, the XTB3F-1 was designed in late 1944 and had its first flight in December 1945. It could carry 2 torpedoes or 4,000 lbs of bombs. The prototype had a Westinghouse 19XB jet tail nozzle intended to boost the XTB3F's top speed to around 356 mph for short bursts, this idea was never tested. The XTB3F-1 was then refitted for anti-submarine search, the jet removed and a large radome fitted in the bomb bay. Thus the XTB3F-1S was born. Out of this arrangement came the AF-2W Guardian.

regular Navy, the Reservists were able to test these ideas; thus enabling the Reservists to keep in touch with newer methods and also train themselves and new pilots on up to date concepts. The Reserve Avengers trained many a pilot and helped to keep the "old pros" sharp.

In 1950, the Reserve program had a chance to prove its worth. When the country of South Korea was invaded by the Communists, many of the Reserve pilots were called to active duty. However, they would not take the Avenger into this conflict, the first of the "brush fire wars". The TBM's were tired and newer aircraft were available. A large number of the Avenger Reserve

TBM-3W in flight 1949.

TBM-3R from Marine Corps Headquarters Squadron One. (HEDRON-1), Korea 1952.

pilots were trained in the new Douglas AD Skyraider before entering into active duty. Several Reserve Units were called up as a complete

NAS Kingsville, Texas TBM-3S2. Squadron is Advanced Training Unit - 400. — Cdr. T. Johnstone.

squadron and assigned to Carriers and Air Groups of the Fleet. They stacked up quite a remarkable record in the next few years and proved that the Reserve program had paid off. Most of the pilots that entered into the Korean conflict were either World War II veterans in the Reserves or Reserve trained.

The TBM-3E was the only Avenger that served in the Reserve program until mid-1952 when the -3Q's and -3N's began to appear. In late 1952, TBM-3's were assigned to the Reserves. However, by the end of March 1956, only 3 of the Avengers remained on the list of Reserve TBM's. Denver had one TBM-3E and Seattle had the remaining two. By the end of 1956, there were none.

The "old Turkey" had now disappeared from the Reserves and the Fleet. However, one lad of so many years ago, will never forget her shinny blue paint job and the gleaming white "U" on her tail as she flew over the tree tops toward a safe landing at the Naval Air Station, St. Louis, Missouri.

TBM-3E used to evacuate wounded Marines in Korea during the early part of the Korean Conflict, 1950.

AVENGER SERVICE
WITH OTHER COUNTRIES

TBF-1C of the RNZAF at Ohakea Station, 1950.   *Photo credit — 'd E. C. Darby.*

Several other countries have used the TBF/M Avenger for either combat service or non-combat service.

The first country to acquire the Avenger from the United States was Great Britain. Under the Lend-Lease plan between the two countries, the first Avengers were delivered to the Fleet Air Arm in 1943. Throughout the remaining years of World War II a total of 978 Avengers found their way into 15 front line squadrons, mainly with the Royal Navy. They served with the British escort and large fleet carriers as well as with land based units on the home front.

When the Avengers arrived in Great Britain their designations assumed a different classification. The TBF-1's became the Tarpon 1, 402 being delivered; the TBM-1 became the Avenger II, 344 delivered and the TBM-1 with special anti-submarine radar installed became the Avenger III, 232 being delivered.

The Avengers of the Royal Navy served in both the Atlantic and Pacific Theaters.

The Pacific based Royal Navy Avengers were involved in many of the same actions as the U. S. Avengers and were involved in rocket, bomb and torpedo attacks against the Japanese Fleet, islands and mainland. In the Atlantic they served mainly as anti-submarine patrol and protection of convoys.

The British pilots felt the same respect for the Avenger as did the service pilots of the United States. Their respect can best be appreciated in the words of a Royal Navy pilot. "JZ300 got her tail singed in a glide bombing attack on enemy shipping in St. Male, France. From 12,000 feet, six Avengers went in at 45 degrees to release their load from 1,000 feet. JZ300 was caught under the tail by shore ack-ack and went on her nose, heading for the water. The pilot, hit in the back, phoned, 'Stand by to ditch.' The observer did not

TBF-1C of #5 Target Tug Squadron of RNZAF at Ohakea Station, 1945. Turkey was painted yellow with black stripes.   Photo credit — 'd E. C. Darby.

TBF-1C on display at Royal New Zealand Air Force Base at Te Rapa, this Turkey last flew in 1959.
Photo credit — 'd E. C. Darby.

2504 before her retirement at Te Rapa. 1959. — 'd E. C. Darby.

answer. He was dead. Somehow the plane, half the tail gone, cockpit shattered, aerials blown off, managed to right herself. Five miles from the coast, in filthy weather, ceiling 200 feet, visibility 1½ miles, the pilot put down the flaps at 120 knots, but there was no feeling in the stick. He still didn't realize he was flying with only half a tail. They crept in round the coast at 150 feet until at last they saw the base. The plane wouldn't drop properly so they floated three quarters of the way down the runway in the darkness. Only when they climbed out did they begin to wonder how they ever got back; port tail and elevator missing, hole of about 5 inches in the remainder of the tail plane, cockpit enclosure shattered, pilot's headrest hit, bulkhead behind the pilot's cockpit shattered by 36 holes."

Truly "The planes you put your trust in," as stated by Sub-Lieutenant (A) Thomas Derrick White, RN-VR, who was the pilot.

In 1949, the Royal Canadian Navy obtained 115 Avengers, TBM-3's, from the United States Navy for use in its' anti-submarine program. With the acquisition of the TBM-3's, Canada increased her air defense system to a level with

Royal Navy TBM-3, 1949.

other countries in the Western Hemisphere and was able to fulfill its role of anti-submarine warfare operations in the North Atlantic. The Avengers were replacing the aging Fireflies, then used by the Canadian Navy. With the arrival of the Avengers, Canada was also able to increase its number of ASW units. The Avengers were also used by the RCN as trainers. Four additional TBM-3W's were later obtained from the United States to give the ASW squadrons additional Airborne Early Warning coverage. The Royal Canadian Navy used the Avenger until 1957; they were once again being replaced by more modern aircraft.

In the early 1950s', the French Navy, Aeronavale, acquired some of the Avengers to bolster its' anti-submarine forces too. Although the exact number of aircraft they received is not known, it is known that they used the TBM-3W-2 and the TBM-3. A few of these aircraft were used by the French forces in the allied attack against Egypt in 1957. As late as 1962, three Avenger Squadrons still remained in service with the Aeronavale and served as shipboard anti-submarine units. The units were the Aeronavale Flottille 4F, 6F and 9F.

In 1953, the Royal Netherlands Naval Air Service received 50 TBM-3s' and -3Ws' which were used to equip two squadrons for anti-submarine duties, and as of 1963, were still being used.

Uruguay also made use of the Avenger when it received a number of TBM-1Cs'. They were being used by the Service Aeronautica de la Marina and served as operational torpedo bombers.

New Zealand has also made use of the Aven-

Photo credit — Gordon Swanborough

Royal Canadian Navy TBM-3, 1950.

Photo credit — Peter Troop

ger by using it as a Tow Target aircraft for anti-aircraft gunnery practice.

In 1955, the Japanese Maritime Self Defense Force began receiving Avengers from the United States. The largest share of the Avengers were TBM-3W-2s' and were specially equipped with radome and anti-submarine electronic sensing equipment. Toward the end of 1955, an additional number of TBM-3S-2s' was delivered to Japan to bolster its' defense force and for use as spare parts.

As the years passed, spare parts were becoming harder to find as many of the old Avengers were being scrapped. The Japanese used the Avenger until 1960, when the few remaining were converted into target towing aircraft. By the end of 1962, the last of the JMSDF Avengers were retired from service.

French Navy TBM-3S aboard the carrier Bois Belleau (ex-USS Belleau Wood CVL-24) in June of 1957.

Photo credit — Fred Freeman

TBM-3S2 of Japanese Maritime Self-Defense Force, 23 July 1962. Photo taken at JMSDF Air Station - Shirai.
Photo credit — Toyokazu Matsuzaki

An interesting fact that should be noteworthy is that the JMSDF did not lose one TBM due to an accident while in its service, 7 years.

Ironic as it seems, the airplane that once helped defeat a Nation was later found in the service of that Nation as a protector of her shores.

* * * * * * * * *

Chapter 6

TODAY

TBM-3 converted to role of fire bomber. Pretty blue, black, gold and white Avenger was between assignments at Van Nuys, California airport, April 1962.
Photo credit — M. J. Kishpaugh

Today, the Avenger is 29 years old and after 14 years of service with the United States Navy and Marine Corps, it can still be found lumbering through the skies; this time in a different capacity.

When the Avenger was deemed no longer useful to the U. S. Navy, due to the advancing air age, it was retired from service and began the long journey to the scrap yards. However, several enterprising businessmen in the United States and British Columbia had developed a use for the TBM's and began to purchase them as war surplus material from the United States and Canadian Governments. Their business was crop dusting, forest spraying, aerial firefighting and reseeding burned out forests.

TBM-1C (N-9394H), USN BuNo. (46122) had its bomb bay modified by Mr. Otto Timm, the bomb bay doors were removed and the bay was lined with a plywood container divided into two tanks with two plywood doors for each tank. Time and engineering costs were saved by using the plywood. The total capacity of this tank came to 600 gallons. To make the units watertight, two 750 kg weather balloons were installed into each compartment, this move also brought down the total cost of the experiment. Four bomb rack shackles secured the tank doors on each pair, toggle switches in the TBM cockpit activated the shackles when release was desired. Upon activa-

tion the tank compartment doors opened and the weight of the water caused the thin rubber balloon linings to burst and the water was released in free fall.

A total of 8 drop tests were made at heights varying from 10' to 100'. The most effective drop proved to be the one made from 50'; it produced a drenched area 90' x 270'.

On 1 September 1954, the Avenger made the first operational bulk water drop ever made in the United States; two drops were made on the Jamison fire.

The testing of many types of aircraft for this new role as aerial firefighters continued from 1954 to 1958 and by 1959 the method of aerial firefighting had been well established.

The United States Forestry Service purchased eight surplus TBM-3U's from the U.S. Navy in 1956 for use as aerial tankers. Registration numbers assigned were: N-102Z thru N-109Z. The first bulk drop made by a USFS Avenger was made at Redding, California on 15 May 1957. The TBM, N-104Z, was fitted with a two compartment 400 gallon tank designed by the California Division of Forestry and built in their shops at Davis, California. N-104Z made the drop at 100' while flying at 115 mph, it formed a swath 50' x 300'.

Improvements were made in the tanks car-

Line up of Avenger fire bombers belonging to Skyway Air Services Ltd., Abbetsford, British Columbia, 1969.

ried by the TBM's until finally it was found that a 600 gallon tank filled the bill for the job intended. The Avenger soon began to appear in the stables of many private contractors, this came about because of the demonstrations given by the USFS in TBM number N-104Z.

From its first flight in 1941 through the 1950's, '60's and on into the '70's, the Avenger is still going strong. A tribute to the fine engineers that designed her, the hard working men and women that built her and the dedicated men that flew her; the Avenger has served well for over 30 years.

THIS TURKEY CAN TRULY FLY.

One of the first companies formed was Jim Venable's Hemet Valley Flying Service, operating from Hemet airport, about 90 miles south of Los Angeles, California. Hemet Valley Flying Service is considered to be one of the best operations in the United States. Venable started in the aerial tanker business in 1958 with two Stearmans. Today, the company operates 10 TBM's and three PBY's (Catalinas) as tankers. Part of this fleet is committed to the state and part to the Federal Government, and is under contract to the United States Forest Service and the California Division of Forestry.

Venable's biggest problem is the maintenance of the aircraft. Spare engines for the TBMs, as well as the PBYs, are non-existent. If any of the engines are damaged, or when overhaul times comes, Venable must pay out $10,000 for the PBY's and $7,000 for the TBM's.

All of Venables aircraft are given a complete check after every four hours of flying time. The TBM's take the heaviest beating and are always subject to a comprehensive preventive maintenance program and required periodic inspections.

The best known Canadian operation is that of Art Sellers' Skyways at Abbottsford, British Col-

umbia. Generally speaking, Skyways is considered to be a twin to Venable's Hemet Valley operation. At present, Sellers operates 14 TBM's, nine of which are under contract and five are used as spares. He is acknowledged to have a complete corner on TBM spares, having purchased the entire Royal Navy inventory of Avengers. Starting about 11 years ago with 18 aircraft, he figures to be good for another 20 years with the TBM's. At present his entire tanker operation strength runs about 40 aircraft.

Since both Venable and Sellers have been operating, their tanker services have each lost four TBM's in 10 years. A remarkable record.

Venable and Sellers, as well as the pilots they employ, freely admit theirs is a high risk business. For the pilot the risk comes in terms of his life. For the operators the risk shows up in the form of small profits and a constant threat of financial ruin.

Aerial firefighting has expanded largely in the last 12 years. Air tanker operations in the United States and Canada has become a $15-million business annually, with more than 200 fixed wing aircraft being employed. Federal and State government authorities consider the air tanker a well established component of its fire fighting force.

At the end of 1969, nearly half of all tankers under contract in the Western United States and British Columbia were TBM's, a total of 66. B-26's were second at 19 and B-17's third at 14. There were 10 F7F twin engine Navy fighter bombers and at least 8 PBY's, 6 B-25's and 7 P4Y's.

So, some 29 years later, the versatile old Avenger is still in operation. Although her present job is far from the one for which she was designed, it is still an important one. No one knows for sure when the last Avenger will depart from the sky, but until that day arrives one can still feel that this magnificent old airplane has served her country well, in war as well as peace.

Avenger 1970   *Photo credit — Larkins*

INFORMATION ABOUT:

SUPPLEMENT
TO
GRUMMAN
T B F / T B M   "AVENGER"

by   B. R. JACKSON and T. E. DOLL

This "SUPPLEMENT" to the basic text of

Aero Series, Volume 21 should prove to

be of paramount value to the historian

and the serious modeler. It covers all

the materials noted here that could not

be included in Volume 21 itself.

32 pages - - - - -$1.95 paperback

TABLE OF CONTENTS

TO: *Aero Publishers, Inc.*   **Order Form**

329 Aviation Road
Fallbrook, California 92028

Please send me _____ copies of "SUPPLEMENT TO GRUMMAN, TBF/TBM "AVENGER,
@ $1.95 each. Please add 25¢ for handling. California residents add 5% sales tax.

NAME _____

ADDRESS _____

CITY _____ STATE _____ ZIP _____

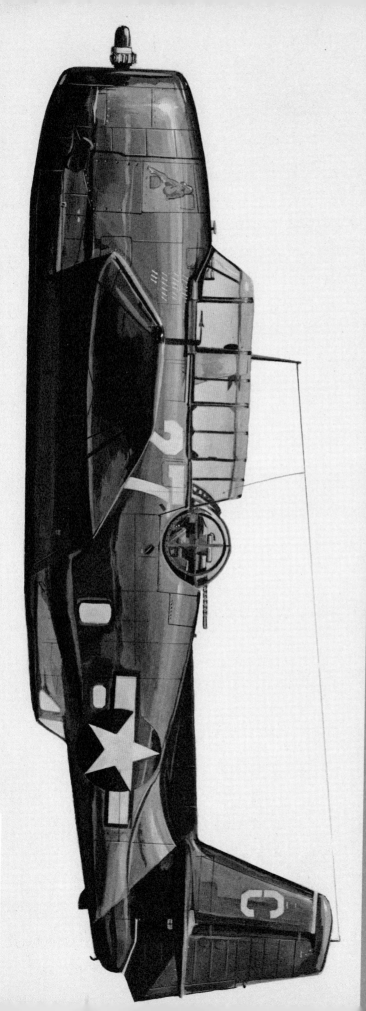

"TBM-1C of VT-28 on the USS MONTEREY CVL-26 during July 1945."

ISBN—0—8168—0580—6